THE
ESTABLISHMENT'S MAN

THE ESTABLISHMENT'S MAN

BY

JAMES J. DRUMMEY

PUBLISHERS

APPLETON, WISCONSIN

Published by
Western Islands
Post Office Box 8040
Appleton, Wisconsin 54913
414-749-3783

Printed in the United States of America
Library of Congress
Catalog Card Number: 90-071487
ISBN: 0-88279-032-3

Contents

About the Author

A graduate of Boston College, James J. Drummey has spent more than 30 years lecturing and writing about American history and government, the threat of communism and socialism, and events of national and international significance. He has been director of research for the John Birch Society and news editor of its affiliated weekly magazine, *The Review Of The News*. Since its founding in 1985, Mr. Drummey has served as senior editor of *The New American*, a biweekly journal of news and opinion also affiliated with the Society. His carefully researched articles on a variety of historical and topical issues have influenced the thinking of a generation of Americans.

Introduction

> *[When making a choice for President], a voter who wants a liberal policy should vote Republican; conversely, if he yearns for a conservative policy, he should cast his ballot for a Democrat.*
> — Thomas Gale Moore, May 1981

One of the greatest paradoxes of our time is the way in which supposedly conservative Republican Presidents have promoted big government and internationalism in the United States. Presidents Eisenhower, Nixon, Reagan, and Bush all talked like conservatives, but the record shows that their policies advanced the liberal agenda at a faster and more ominous clip than any Democratic occupants of the White House could have done.

Americans have repeatedly become disenchanted with Republican Presidents who abandoned their campaign promises and moved to the left. But these frustrated voters have usually consoled themselves by saying, "Well, at least the country is better off than if Adlai Stevenson were President." Or Hubert Humphrey, George McGovern, Jimmy Carter, Walter Mondale, and Michael Dukakis. But is the country better off?

Supporters of Governor Dukakis in the 1988 campaign are now chiding George Bush for adopting many of the Democratic nominee's liberal views. And there is no doubt that Mr. Bush has been able to get away with policies that would have gotten Dukakis in serious trouble, such as inviting homosexual activists to the White House, appeasing Red Chinese tyrant Deng Xiaoping, or fawning over South African terrorist Nelson Mandela.

In the early days of the Reagan Administration, researcher Thomas Gale Moore of the Hoover Institution at Stanford University published the results of a study demonstrating that a Republican in the White House would do more for the liberal cause than a Democrat. He documented his thesis with some startling statistics drawn from an analysis of four Republican and four Democratic administrations.

Factors such as "party loyalty" and the enormous power of a sitting President to reward or punish congressional members of his party offer partial explanations for the phenomenon. But why Republican Presidents have been so much more successful in achieving liberal objectives than Democrats is not the issue here. We are more concerned with Moore's overall conclusion.

He is not the first to discover such a pattern. Back in 1957, at the midpoint of the Eisenhower Administration, six-time Socialist Party candidate for President Norman Thomas enthused that "the United States is making greater strides toward socialism under Eisenhower than even under Roosevelt." Thirteen years later, during the Nixon Administration, liberal Republican Senator Hugh Scott of Pennsylvania gleefully asserted: "We [liberals] get the action and conservatives get the rhetoric."

One example from the Reagan Administration will serve to illustrate that liberals do indeed get the action while conservatives are soothed with rhetoric. During his Inaugural Address on January 20, 1981, President Reagan said of the economic crisis then facing the nation: "Government is not the solution to our problem; government is the problem."

This fundamentally sound conservative position hit the nail right on the head. Its rhetorical impact as Mr. Reagan began his Presidency was immense, but conservative action did not follow. Where widespread cuts in socialistic programs were expected, the new President announced only three weeks later that he was merely "reducing the rate of increase" in taxing and spending. And this is precisely how the Reagan Administration addressed the nation's economic crisis. Despite shrieks of horror from bureaucrats and redistribute-the-wealth partisans about alleged cutbacks, government continued to grow.

Then, in his 1983 State of the Union speech, Mr. Reagan reversed his rhetoric as well. Reciting from the liberal creed, he declared: "We who are in government must take the lead in restoring the economy." Congressional big spenders, led by Speaker of the House "Tip" O'Neill, roared their approval of the President's turnaround, and government intervention in the lives of the American people grew at an even faster pace.

In the process, the Republican President's 1980 campaign promises to abolish the Department of Education and do away with the Department of Energy were only two of the casualties. Liberal actions had triumphed even though the early conservative rhetoric continued to receive media attention and continued to disarm properly concerned Americans.

In this important book, James J. Drummey shows from a wide variety of sources that President George Bush has likewise adopted the agenda of the left, angering conservatives and delighting liberals, socialists, and one-worlders. Like his Republican predecessors in the White House, Mr. Bush has fragmented Republican opposition to more government and more foreign entanglements. And he has earned the plaudits of those internationalists in and out of government whose credentials include membership in the unelected but extremely powerful clique known as the "Establishment."

For many decades, Establishment-connected politicians, diplomats, industrialists, and others have tightened their grip on America. A careful study of their history shows that their goal is not benign rule under a more liberal but tolerable administration of power. Rather, if they have their way, they will cancel the American dream. National sovereignty will be replaced by one-world government; individual economic freedom will fall victim to Big Brother-style domination of the many by the few; and the American people will discover that their greatest enemy has sprung from within.

All of this doesn't have to happen. The internal forces arrayed against America can be defeated by an aroused, well-informed, and determined citizenry.

This carefully researched and temperately written book does not purport to look into the mind of George Bush. But it does examine his record as it has been chronicled by his own words and deeds, and as it has been assessed by an array of commentators from both the conservative and liberal points on the political spectrum.

The conclusion reached by Mr. Drummey is that George Bush is indeed "The Establishment's Man." Accordingly, this book should contribute mightily to the much-needed informing and arousing of the sleeping giant known as the American people.

— John F. McManus
Publisher, Western Islands
November 1, 1990

THE
ESTABLISHMENT'S
MAN

The word "Establishment" is a general term for the power elite in international finance, business, the professions and government, largely from the northeast, who wield most of the power regardless of who is in the White House. Most people are unaware of the existence of this "legitimate Mafia." Yet the power of the Establishment makes itself felt from the professor who seeks a foundation grant, to the candidate for a Cabinet post or State Department job. It affects the nation's policies in almost every area.

— Edith Kermit Roosevelt

Prologue

If President Bush does a lot of things Democrats want done and does them reasonably well, why would you want to beat him?
— Governor Mario Cuomo of New York
as quoted in *Human Events*, April 28, 1990

A *New York Times*/CBS poll conducted at the end of George Bush's first year in the White House found that three out of four Americans interviewed approved of the President's handling of the nation's affairs. It was the highest approval rating any President had received since John F. Kennedy's 79 percent in January 1962. On the surface at least, the high regard shown for Mr. Bush should have come as no surprise. After all, here was a man who had been a war hero, a successful businessman, a Congressman, our country's ambassador to the United Nations, chairman of the Republican National Committee, an envoy to Communist China, director of the Central Intelligence Agency, Vice President for eight years, and the choice of nearly 48 million voters in the 1988 election, enough to capture the electoral votes of 40 states on the way to becoming the 41st President of the United States.

His inaugural address on January 20, 1989, sounded all the proper themes. It opened with a prayer for heavenly guidance; proclaimed that "the totalitarian era is passing" and a new breeze of freedom is blowing across the globe; called for replacing the obsessive quest for material gains with the pursuit of "high moral principle" on the way to making "kinder the face of the nation and gentler the face of the world"; vowed to keep America strong enough to protect peace in the world while at the same time continuing "our new closeness with the Soviet Union"; and invited the American people to join in writing a new chapter in their history — "a small and stately story of unity, diversity, and generosity, shared and written together."

The year that followed saw the President put many of these themes into practice. On the domestic scene, he proposed or supported a number of initiatives purportedly designed to help in the areas of drug control, education, the environment, civil rights, housing, and the minimum wage. On the international front, he engineered the ouster of Manuel Noriega in Panama, welcomed new governments in the communist-occupied nations of Europe and urged U.S. aid for them, recommended various disarmament initiatives, and frequently expressed his support for Mikhail Gorbachev's program of restructuring known as perestroika, even traveling to the Mediterranean island of Malta in December 1989 for a meeting with the Soviet ruler.

The only foreign venture that generated any major criticism for Mr. Bush during his first year in office was his attempt to maintain good relations with Red China after the June 1989 massacre of thousands of student demonstrators in Tiananmen Square. But not even that effort, which included a secret trip by Bush aides to Beijing only one month after the massacre, had any lasting negative impact on the President's popularity.

The State of the Union

So when he delivered his State of the Union address on January 31, 1990, President Bush was optimistic about the future. He spoke enthusiastically about the "Revolution of '89" in Central and Eastern Europe and called it a validation of an American policy "based on a single, shining principle:

the cause of freedom." He challenged Americans to make their nation a better place for all, to anchor themselves to the pillars of "faith and family," and to "affirm our allegiance to this idea we call America. And let us all remember that the State of the Union depends on each and every one of us."

Thoughtful listeners to the President's message were not quite so optimistic. They found some of his remarks to be downright inaccurate. For instance, Mr. Bush said that his new $1.2 trillion budget "brings federal spending under control," and he predicted a balanced budget by 1993. But spending was hardly "under control" when the Administration was then estimating the deficit for fiscal 1991 at $63 billion and, by October 1990, had jumped its estimate to $294 billion! And that figure did not include the cost of bailing out the savings and loan industry, which was expected to add another $62 billion to the 1991 deficit.

Mr. Bush said that he wanted "not more bureaucracy, not more red tape," but in the same breath he called for elevating the Environmental Protection Agency to Cabinet status and giving it an additional $2 billion "to protect our environment." He also talked about clean air, child care, excellence in education, farm bills, transportation policy, product liability reform, health care, crime, and drug abuse. Some of these issues have already generated large bureaucracies and mountains of red tape. The new and expanded programs he discussed can only lead to the exact opposite of his promise of "not more bureaucracy, not more red tape."

"For more than 40 years," the President went on to say, "America and its allies held communism in check." That will come as news to the captive peoples of China, Tibet, Cambodia, Laos, Vietnam, North Korea, Afghanistan, Angola, Mozambique, Ethiopia, Zimbabwe, Cuba, Nicaragua, and other nations which fell to the cruel forces of totalitarian communism during the more than four decades referred to by Mr. Bush.

His statement in that January 31st address about a "free Poland" where members of the Solidarity trade union were leading the Polish government amounted to more stretching of the truth. There were indeed some members of Solidarity in the Polish government. But its real leaders at that time — all communists — were President Wojciech Jaruzelski, Interior Minister Czeslaw Kiszczak, Defense Minister Florian Siwicki, and Transportation Minister Adam Wieladek. These and other communists continued to control the police, the secret police, the military, and a great deal of Poland's infrastructure. Hardline communist Jaruzelski retained the power to dismiss Solidarity member Tadeusz Mazowiecki as Prime Minister, dissolve Parliament, and declare martial law.

Calling Poland a "free" country in January 1990 was akin to claiming that black is white. Even when Mazowiecki ousted Kiszczak, Siwicki, and Wieladek from the government in July 1990, the communists remained in control of the nation.

The Adaptable Man

George Bush has often described himself as a conservative. "I am a conservative who believes in the idea of limited government," he said in an interview published in the January 1986 issue of the now-defunct *Conservative Digest*. He also said that "it is not government's role to confiscate and redistribute the hard-earned treasure of those who have worked for a living," that "our Constitution limits the role for government, and I feel very strongly about decentralization," and that "conservatism in this age should be equated with a realistic view of communist intentions and a realistic view of communist governments."

Yet the policies he promoted during his first 20 months as President were quite the opposite of the views he expressed in the pages of the *Conservative Digest*. This dichotomy has led increasing numbers of Americans, liberals as well as conservatives, to express doubts about the alleged conservatism of Mr. Bush. "To many conservatives," said Walter Robinson in the *Boston Globe*, "President Bush seems to have no ideological soul." Maureen Dowd of the *New York Times* summed up Mr. Bush's first year in the White House in these words: "His principles are unwavering on public service, family, and loyalty, but adaptable on nearly everything else."

Describing the President as "adaptable" may be accurate as long as it is understood that he usually adapts to positions favored by leftists and internationalists, even while expressing opposing viewpoints. Since this places him in conformity with a predominantly leftist and internationalist media, Mr. Bush's first-year popularity was hardly surprising. But such a chameleon-like approach to matters of great importance to America and the Free World is worrying many Americans. "There is growing concern about the direction of the Bush Administration," said Howard Phillips, chairman of The Conservative Caucus. "More and more conservatives are talking about it as the Nelson Rockefeller Administration that never was."

The President's invitation to homosexual activists to be present at the White House for the signing of the Hate Crimes Statistics Act, and his charges of censorship against those opposing taxpayer funding of pornographic and anti-Christian "art" led *National Review* to headline an editorial, "George Dukakis." Columnist Patrick J. Buchanan declared that the guideposts of the Bush Administration "seem to be old position papers left around the offices of David Rockefeller's Trilateral Commission."

Human Events, the conservative Washington weekly, accused the Bush Administration of "blurring the differences" between the Republican and Democratic parties. Noting that the President had gone along with the Clean Air Act, the elevation of the EPA to Cabinet status, the Americans with Disabilities Act, National Endowment for the Arts funding of obscene "art," and Democratic proposals to raise $200 billion in new taxes, *Human Events* asked: "Where, in fact, is he drawing substantive differences with the Democrats these days? No place of great significance."

A Dukakis Clone

All of this is not surprising, said columnist Joseph Sobran, because "for George Bush, conservatism isn't a philosophy; it's a special interest, to be appeased occasionally." Sobran said that "conservatives supported George Bush in 1988 because he presented himself as Reagan's successor, a polar opposite to Michael Dukakis. But it turns out that Bush is likely to give us just about everything we'd have suffered under Dukakis."

In fact, as Sobran wrote in May of 1990, Mr. Bush had courted so many liberal lobbies that he no longer deserved conservative support:

> To support Bush at this point is to acquiesce not only in these separate wrongs and deceits, but also in the conversion of the U.S. into what amounts to a one-party system.... Bush's wooly logic tells him that conservatives have nowhere else to go. He thinks they see it this way, too. What needs to be impressed on him is that as long as he offers no substantial alternative to the Democrats, conservative logic dictates that supporting him is actually worse than letting the Democrats win.

Bushwatcher Gary Benoit believes that the President has only pretended to be a conservative throughout his career so as to advance a "socialist-internationalist agenda in the name of conservatism." Writing in the February 26, 1990 issue of *The New American*, Benoit pointed out that while George Bush in 1988 accused Michael Dukakis of being "far outside the mainstream" and of espousing a philosophy that was similar to the "socialistic, high-controlled experience" of other nations, "the philosophical differences between Mr. Bush and Mr. Dukakis were far less substantive than their campaign rhetoric suggested."

According to Benoit, the two candidates actually held common policy objectives, which were summarized in a September 4, 1988 article in the *Los Angeles Times*:

> Private conversation within both campaigns is increasingly about a new world order in which the Soviet-American conflict is rapidly receding and in which economic issues seem ever more intractable to either party's traditional solutions. But voters are unlikely to hear much on either point.

George Wallace's comment in 1968 that there "isn't a dime's worth of difference" between the Republican and Democratic parties certainly applies with George Bush in the White House. The attitude of Mr. Bush and his alter ego, James Baker, is one of "split the difference," said Maureen Dowd and Thomas L. Friedman in the May 6, 1990 *New York Times Magazine*. "If what seems reasonable at the moment is to side with the Chinese power elite rather than the students in Tiananmen Square, then you side with those in power. If what seems reasonable is to split the difference between the aspirations of Lithuanians and the interests of Gorbachev, then you split the difference."

Siding with tyrants in Beijing and Moscow is not really splitting the difference, of course; it is adapting to the desires of the extreme left.

Using Dan Quayle

Or you try to appease conservatives by having someone like Vice President Dan Quayle, who came to the office with relatively good conservative credentials, play the "good-cop, bad-cop" routine regarding the intentions of Mikhail Gorbachev. While Mr. Bush appealed to liberals and moderates with the statement in his 1989 Thanksgiving Message that "there is no greater advocate of perestroika than the President of the United States," Mr. Quayle had tried to soothe conservatives a few weeks earlier. He called Gorbachev "an ideological Leninist" and said that the Soviet rulers "still have expansionary attitudes in Central America, Afghanistan, Ethiopia, Cambodia, and elsewhere."

Asked about these conflicting statements, Quayle spokesman David Beckwith replied: "What the Vice President is doing is articulating a part of U.S. policy: differences with the Soviet Union. You can call it a difference in tonal quality. We're all singing from the same songbook, but there are different parts." The more likely explanation is that the Administration was trying to reassure Republicans who are uncomfortable with the President's continuous gushing over Gorbachev.

That kind of strategy is offensive to conservatives like L. Brent Bozell III. "What they are saying then," according to Bozell, "is that Bush will state policy and Quayle will throw the bones to the rabid right to keep us at bay. We don't have any use for that."

Pretty soon, however, the President's liberal views became so engrained in people's wishful thinking, thanks in large measure to the bias of the media, that it was no longer necessary for the Vice President to toss bones to anyone on the right. Asked in February 1990 if he were still suspicious of Gorbachev's intentions, Mr. Quayle responded: "A lot of things have happened, and I have a different assessment of where the Soviet Union is heading and where it may or may not go than I did six months or a year ago."

That it is Mr. Quayle who has changed, and not Gorbachev, will be made clear later in the book. What will also become clear is that George Bush never really had authentic conservative credentials. Oh, there were times when he called himself a conservative, and when he even sounded like a conservative, but more often than not he has promoted the liberal-socialist agenda. The end result of that agenda will be the destruction of our constitutional Republic and the loss of the personal freedoms that made America great.

This book is written to alert concerned Americans to the collectivist-communist-socialist tide that threatens to engulf their country and to George Bush's role in riding rather than stemming that tide. We hope and pray that the information assembled in this book will help to halt the drive for a "new world order" before it is too late.

Mario Cuomo said
Mr. Bush does the things
Democrats want done.

Dan Quayle has tried to
soothe conservatives
upset with Mr. Bush.

Michael Dukakis was
hurt in the campaign by
ties to the ACLU.

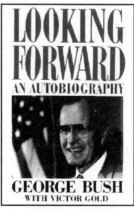

George Bush claimed to
be a conservative in his
1987 autobiography.

Chapter 1
The Careerist

Bush is the favorite son of the Eastern Establishment, the political heir of the late Nelson Rockefeller.
— Steve Neal of the *Chicago Tribune* as quoted in *American Opinion*, September 1980

If there is one constant in the public life of George Herbert Walker Bush, it is his lifelong association with the Eastern Establishment. He has always been at home with that enormously influential coterie of bankers, foundation heads, Ivy League graduates, media moguls, and liberal politicians usually found holding membership in such internationalist-minded organizations as the Council on Foreign Relations and the Trilateral Commission. The epitome of Eastern Establishmentarianism for many years was Nelson Rockefeller, the former governor of New York and perennial presidential candidate of the Eastern wing of the Republican Party. Though his White House ambitions were never realized, Rockefeller served as an appointed Vice President under Gerald Ford from 1974 to 1977.

When Rockefeller-style Republicans were searching in 1980 for someone to block the nomination of Ronald Reagan, their eagerness for George Bush was obvious. He was the "perfect Old Boy Network careerist" and the candidate of the Eastern Establishment, claimed political commentator Kevin Phillips at the time. Liberal David Nyhan of the *Boston Globe* agreed, saying that "Bush brings an Eastern Establishment cachet with him: his candidacy was endorsed by moderates like Henry Cabot Lodge, Elliot Richardson, and William

Ruckelshaus." (It is worth noting that only from the *Globe*'s far-left perspective would Lodge, Richardson, and Ruckelshaus seem like moderates.)

Although George Bush has maintained a voting address in Houston, Texas, for more than three decades, he has spent most of those years serving in a variety of government posts in Washington. For some, his Texas connection may have obscured the fact that he was born in Massachusetts, raised in Connecticut, and educated in both of those states, graduating in 1948 from Yale University, where he was a member in his senior year of the exclusive and secretive Skull and Bones society.

His father, Prescott Bush, a managing partner of the Wall Street international banking firm of Brown Brothers, Harriman, served as a liberal Republican U.S. Senator from Connecticut from 1953 to 1962. After distinguishing himself as a Navy pilot in World War II, flying 58 combat missions and being rescued by a submarine after his plane was shot down in September 1944, George Bush married Barbara Pierce, daughter of the publisher of *Redbook* and *McCall*'s magazines, in 1945.

Following his graduation from Yale, George declined an offer to join Brown Brothers, Harriman and went to work for Dresser Industries, selling oil drilling bits in Texas and California. He and a partner formed their own oil and gas company in Midland, Texas, in 1950. This firm was absorbed three years later by the Zapata Petroleum Corporation. In 1954, Bush co-founded and became president of the Zapata Offshore Company, a developer of offshore drilling equipment. He transferred Zapata Offshore's headquarters and his home to Houston in 1959.

Republican Politics

In the early 1960s, Bush became involved in Texas Republican Party politics and agreed to run for Harris County

Republican chairman to prevent a member of the John Birch Society from getting that job. "It was clear that a John Birch Society takeover of the Harris County party would mean that all the gains Republicans had made in recent years would be jeopardized," Bush wrote in his 1987 autobiography *Looking Forward*. He said that "the campaign would be tough because the Birchites were well-organized and zealous. Whoever ran for county chairman against their candidate would have to work overtime, touring the county, visiting every precinct, making speeches every night for several weeks."

But George was up to the challenge, and he was elected county chairman for a period of two years. "By the end of 1963, our membership had grown and we'd raised enough money to move the headquarters to a better location," he said. "The Birchites were still grumbling, but that was another lesson I carried over from my experience in business: You can't keep everybody happy." It would not be the last time that Bush would intervene to keep conservative, anti-communist Americans from positions of influence.

In 1964, Bush was persuaded to run against incumbent U.S. Senator Ralph Yarborough. He supported the presidential candidacy of Barry Goldwater, called for arming anti-Castro exiles, demanded U.S. withdrawal from the United Nations if it admitted Communist China, said that a federal medical care program would "overburden the Social Security system and would lead to socialized medicine," declared that the 1963 Test Ban Treaty was "not a legitimate step toward peace," and denounced the Civil Rights Act of 1964 as a measure designed "to usurp the rights of the people."

The rookie candidate did not win, but he got a respectable 43.5 percent of the vote against Yarborough, who, ironically, had described Bush as "the darling of the John Birch Society."

In a campaign post-mortem that appeared in the December 1, 1964 issue of *National Review*, Bush blamed Goldwater's loss to Lyndon Johnson (and presumably his own defeat) on "nut-fringe" zealots who would pounce on undecided voters "with an anti-LBJ book or an inflammatory pamphlet" and push their views in a way that "scared the hell out of the plain average non-issue-conscious man on the street." And in his 1987 autobiography, he ridiculed those who in 1964 had raised the issue of support for him by persons affiliated with the Council on Foreign Relations, which he said some voters felt was "nothing more than a One World tool of the Communist-Wall Street internationalist conspiracy."

Two Terms in Congress

George Bush's next attempt at political office was more successful. In 1966, he captured a seat in the House of Representatives from the Seventh Congressional District in Texas. He was reelected without opposition in 1968. During his four years in Congress, Bush moved progressively to the left. His voting score, according to the moderately conservative Americans for Constitutional Action, declined from 83 percent conservative in 1967 to 58 percent in 1970.

As the Congressman from Houston, he voted against food stamps, forced busing to achieve school desegregation, and wage and price controls. He supported the House Committee on Internal Security and prayer in the schools. Those were positions favored by conservatives. But he was also frequently found backing liberal "solutions" to the nation's problems. For instance, he consistently voted for measures to expand the federal government's controls, including the Consumer Product Safety Commission, the Occupational Safety and Health Act (OSHA), the Environmental Protection Agency, and the federal Office of Education. When President Nixon vetoed the education proposal, Bush voted to override the veto. (The Constitution gives the federal government no authority to involve itself in the field of education. But the absence of any such authority apparently never bothered the future President.)

Congressman Bush voted for the Civil Rights Act of 1968, which contained a highly controversial "open housing" provision stripping property owners of their right to sell or rent to whom they chose. He supported "War on Poverty" transfer-of-wealth schemes; opposed a constitutional amendment to protect the unborn against abortion; co-sponsored the Equal Rights Amendment, which legal scholars believe would have prohibited laws against abortion on the grounds of sex discrimination and given the federal government greater powers; drafted a measure proposing establishment of a congressional Joint Select Committee on Population and Family Planning; and co-sponsored legislation to expand government birth control programs.

As a Congressman, George Bush also voted for the Gun Control Act of 1968, which prohibited interstate shipment of rifles, shotguns, and ammunition and restricted out-of-state purchases of rifles and shotguns. Criticized for that vote in New Hampshire during the 1980 presidential campaign, Bush said that he was a foe of gun control and only voted for the 1968 act because it contained a provision that set mandatory sentences for persons convicted of committing a crime with a firearm. What he did not say, however, was that the mandatory sentencing provision had been cut from the bill prior to final passage. Only the gun control sections were enacted into law.

In 1970, at the urging of President Nixon, Bush gave up his safe congressional seat to try once again for the Senate seat held by Ralph Yarborough. Bush might well have won this time, but the liberal Yarborough lost the Democratic primary to the less liberal Lloyd Bentsen, who proceeded to garner 54 percent of the vote in the general election to 46 percent for Bush.

UN, Red China, CIA

Mr. Nixon did not forget Bush, however, and named him Ambassador to the United Nations in December 1970. His 21 months at the UN were relatively uneventful except for his role in expelling the Free Chinese government on Taiwan and bringing Red China into the world body. That role is discussed elsewhere in the book. Much of the Ambassador's time was spent defending the UN before an increasingly disenchanted American public. While touting the UN was laborious, it turned out to be an easier task than his next assignment, defending President Richard Nixon from Watergate-related charges while serving as chairman of the Republican National Committee.

On being formally elected GOP national chairman in January 1973, George Bush said, "I do not intend to be some kind of ideological spokesman for all Republicans. It is our party that believes in federalism and it is our party that must welcome diversity." Those should have been easy years for Bush in the wake of Nixon's landslide victory over George McGovern in 1972, but the Watergate fiasco was about to topple the President.

Bush steadfastly defended Nixon through the spring of 1974, when he admitted that he was "deeply troubled" by the "amorality of tone" in the President's taped conversations. He said that his job was "extremely tough" because he was called a Nixon apologist if he defended the President and a turncoat if he failed to do so. His tightrope act came to an end with Nixon's resignation as President on August 9, 1974.

As a reward for his loyalty, President Gerald Ford let Bush pick his next assignment, and the already much travelled careerist chose to become chief of the U.S. Liaison Office in Red China. In his 1987 autobiography, Bush maintained that he wanted to get far away from the "political nightmare" of the final months of the Nixon Administration. So he and Barbara decided to "head for the Far East," as he put it. He managed to overlook Red China's barbarism as he described his motives for choosing to fraternize with history's worst mass murderers:

An important, coveted post like London or Paris would be good for the resume, but Beijing was a challenge, a journey into the unknown. A new China was emerging, and the relationship between the United States and the People's Republic would be crucial in the years to come, not just in terms of Asian but of worldwide American policy.

The appointment did not require Senate confirmation since no formal diplomatic relations existed between the two governments, and the Bushes arrived in what was then called Peking in October 1974. U.S. policy toward the communist regime was firmly in the hands of Henry Kissinger and Bush did little more than preside over the 226-person mission until December 1975, when President Ford called him back to Washington to direct the Central Intelligence Agency.

After receiving Gerald Ford's promise not to make George Bush his running mate in the 1976 presidential election, the Senate confirmed Bush as CIA Director in January 1976. He served in the post until Jimmy Carter entered the White House in January 1977 and is credited with restoring the morale of the intelligence community after congressional investigations had revealed abuses of power under previous directors.

While at the CIA, Bush invited an outside team of specialists to assess the intentions of the Soviet Union after the agency's own analysts had painted what he felt was too rosy a picture of Soviet aims. According to Air Force Intelligence chief Major General George J. Keegan Jr., the outside team concluded that the USSR had taken "a significant lead over the United States" in military might. "American strategy is premised on the principle of war avoidance," said Keegan, "while that of the Soviet Union is premised on war winning." Yet the CIA analysts who had promoted a far softer view of Soviet intentions remained in place and continued to promote that view.

The 1980 Campaign

Returning to Houston early in 1977, Bush got together in the fall of that year with James A. Baker III, who had managed Gerald Ford's unsuccessful 1976 campaign against Jimmy Carter. The two began to make plans for a Bush run for the White House in 1980. He announced his candidacy on May 1, 1979, promising "a new candor" and "the principled, stable leadership we must have in the decade of the eighties." But the only high point in his campaign was a victory in the Iowa caucuses in January 1980. Despite good media coverage, especially when he termed Ronald Reagan's tax-reduction proposals "voodoo economics," Bush was able to win only six primaries, and he terminated his campaign on May 26th. The final count at the Republican Convention gave Reagan 1,580 delegates, Bush 253, and John Anderson 51.

When former President Gerald Ford refused Ronald Reagan's curious offer to be his running mate (their staffs could not agree on how responsibilities might be divided between the two men), Reagan turned to Bush at the GOP Convention in Detroit that summer, and George accepted the invitation immediately. "Although Reagan had some misgivings, logic demanded Bush's selection," said the 1983 edition of *Current Biography*. "He had the relative youth and foreign policy experience that Reagan lacked, and his stands on social issues would make the ticket more acceptable to moderates." The reference to social issues presumably meant Bush's support for the original Equal Rights Amendment and his approval of abortion "in cases of rape, incest, or when the life of the mother is at stake."

At the convention, conservatives who had labored for a Reagan nomination and who wanted no part of the liberal policies of George Bush described Reagan's choice of Bush for his running mate as a betrayal of their efforts.

Bush campaigned hard for the Republican ticket in 1980, even traveling to Communist China in August to reassure the

Reds that Reagan's comments about restoring official U.S. ties with Free China, which had been severed with U.S. recognition of the Peking regime in 1979, were not serious, but were only phrases used "out of habit." Reagan and Bush captured 44 states in November and the new Administration took office the following January.

The Baker Influence

If Ronald Reagan's choice of George Bush for Vice President had disturbed many conservatives, his selection of James Baker as White House chief of staff added to their concern. Baker, who would later become Secretary of the Treasury under Reagan and Secretary of State under Bush, was neither a Reaganite nor a believer in the conservative principles enunciated by Mr. Reagan. "Baker's every action radiates weakness," said John Lofton, then the editor of *Conservative Digest*. "He wants to say 'sorry' to Tip O'Neill, 'sorry' to Brezhnev.... Baker is draining all the blood out of Ronald Reagan."

Reagan loyalists at *Human Events* accused Baker of constantly striving "to moderate the President's policies on economics, defense, foreign affairs, East-West trade, and so forth," and of putting liberal Republicans in key positions. For instance, Baker chose as his deputy Richard Darman, who was described by *Time* magazine as "Reagan's left-hand man." A protege of liberal Republican Elliot Richardson, Darman was portrayed by conservative columnist Stanton Evans as a man who "has frequently gone on record expressing his doubts about conservative ideas and programs." Yet, said Evans, "this is the man who is positioned outside the Oval Office, deciding what information will or will not be sent in to the President." (Darman became President Bush's director of the Office of Management and Budget in 1989.)

Not only did the Bush people bring their own into the Reagan Administration, they also worked to exclude "dedicated conservatives," said Morton Blackwell, a former aide to Reagan. He said that "every Reaganite in government has a collection of horror stories about Bush's people." And supporters of the Vice President (known as "Bushwhackers") leaked stories to the media and helped to force out of the Administration such conservatives as Richard Allen, the President's national security advisor, and Lyn Nofziger, who gave Mr. Reagan political advice. Stan Evans said that it was "the first political purge in history in which a President's initially victorious supporters were systematically liquidated by his defeated opponents."

The Vice President

During his first term as Vice President, Mr. Bush visited 48 states and 59 foreign countries. He praised Filipino President Ferdinand Marcos in 1981 for his "adherence to democratic principles" and said, "We stand with you, sir.… We will not leave you in isolation.… It would be turning our backs on history if we did." Five years later, only weeks after Filipino voters had reelected Marcos, the Reagan Administration pressured him to abdicate and backed Corazon Aquino as his successor.

After the October 1983 terror bombing that killed 239 U.S. Marines in Lebanon, Bush visited Beirut and declared that the Administration was "not going to let a bunch of insidious terrorist cowards shape the foreign policy of the United States." He said that "there will be no slackening of the resolve to do what we intended to do.… We are not going to let our friends down because of terror." But nothing was ever done to ferret out and punish those terrorists.

On the domestic scene, the Vice President was given a variety of assignments, including head of the National Security Council's "crisis management team" and chairman of task forces on regulatory relief, assistance to local authorities probing child murders in Atlanta, and drug smuggling in south

Florida. His willingness to carry out any and every task given him by the President kept him on the ticket in 1984, when Mr. Reagan swamped Walter Mondale. The stage was being set for Bush to succeed President Reagan in 1988.

On October 12, 1987, George Bush declared his candidacy for the Republican presidential nomination and had little trouble securing the endorsement of his party. He came out of the convention well behind Democratic candidate Michael Dukakis in the polls, but once he zeroed in on such issues as the Dukakis-backed furlough program for convicted murderers in Massachusetts and the Dukakis membership in the far-left American Civil Liberties Union, the tide turned and the Bush-Quayle ticket won 40 states in the November election.

Two months before the election, Mr. Bush had indicated that he would not pursue a tough foreign policy in dealing with communists by announcing the creation of a national security task force co-chaired by accommodationists Gerald Ford, Henry Kissinger, Brent Scowcroft, and Zbigniew Brzezinski. This foreshadowing was not lost on Soviet Foreign Minister Eduard Shevardnadze, who visited Bush in September 1988 and subtly endorsed him by telling reporters afterwards that the Vice President had been "involved in all high-level discussions here in Washington at our talks with the President." In the same month, Red Chinese dictator Deng Xiaoping told Secretary of Defense Frank Carlucci, "I hope he [Bush] will be victorious in the election."

Mr. Bush has done nothing as President to disappoint the hopes of Deng and Shevardnadze.

Ralph Yarborough beat
George Bush in a 1964
Senate battle in Texas.

Prescott Bush was both
an international banker
and a Republican Senator.

Stanton Evans accused
Mr. Bush of purging
genuine conservatives.

A younger George Bush
served two terms as a
Texas Congressman.

President Nixon named Bush as U.S. Ambassador to the United Nations.

President Ford let Bush choose his assignment to Communist China.

Even though George Bush had expressed liberal views in his campaign for the GOP nomination, Ronald Reagan chose Bush as his running mate.

Barbara Bush has given
legitimacy to activists
for homosexual rights.

Geraldine Ferraro was Mr.
Bush's Vice-Presidential
rival in the 1984 race.

Mayor Tamsanqa Linda
told Americans the truth
about terrorist Mandela.

Senator Jesse Helms led
efforts to block federal
funding of obscene art.

Chapter 2
The Pragmatist

In the Reagan years, the intellectual conservatives at the Heritage Foundation scorned Bush and Baker as chameleons without true convictions. Now the two pragmatists are out of the closet, plying their let's-make-a-deal brand of politics around the globe.

— Maureen Dowd and Thomas L. Friedman
in the *New York Times Magazine*, May 6, 1990

Although the term "mugwump" was originally applied a century ago to describe reform Republicans who had bolted the Republican Party after the nomination of James G. Blaine for President in 1884, the word has also been used to describe politicians who straddle the issues, "with their mug on one side of the fence and their wump on the other." George Bush has earned the term "mugwump" since he first sought the Presidency in 1980, sometimes switching positions on issues and other times coming down on both sides of a single issue in the same speech.

For instance, Mr. Bush traveled to Oregon in May 1990 to speak at a fundraising breakfast and found himself in the middle of a hot dispute between the logging industry and environmentalists. A commission had recommended that logging be banned in 8.4 million acres of forest in the Northwest to protect the spotted owl, which becomes easier prey for the great horned owl as the forests are thinned out. Those who depend on logging for their livelihood felt that their jobs were more important than the spotted owl.

What position would Mr. Bush take? Well, he started out

on the side of the loggers, declaring, "I reject those who would ignore the economic consequences of the spotted owl decision. The jobs of many thousands of Oregonians and whole communities are at stake." But, he went on to say, "I also reject those who do not recognize their obligation to protect our delicate ecosystem. Common sense tells us to find a needed balance." He told each side what it wanted to hear. Mugwumpery in all its splendor!

Granted, Mr. Bush did not act differently than scores of contemporary politicians faced with a similar situation. But this pragmatic approach to important, even vital, matters wears thin after a while. Consider the President's less-than-consistent views on the following issues and a definite pattern can be detected.

Abortion

As already noted, Mr. Bush in 1980 supported taxpayer funding of abortion in cases of rape, incest, and the life of the mother, and said during his campaign for the nomination, "I do not favor a constitutional amendment to repeal the Supreme Court decision in that regard." In September 1984, the Vice President said that he could not recall making exceptions for using federal funds in cases of rape, incest, and the life of the mother. "My recollection is never supporting federal funding," he said. "But if there is some *Washington Post* quote, we'll have to go back and take a look. But the point is now — not the history of it — but now. I don't support it. Didn't then. Don't now."

A month later, during a debate with Democratic vice presidential candidate Geraldine Ferraro, Mr. Bush said that there had been "an evolution in my position. There has been 15 million abortions since 1973. And I don't take that lightly. There has been a million and a half this year. The President and I do favor a human life amendment. I favor one that would have an exception for incest and rape, and he doesn't, but we both ... only for the life of the mother, and I agree with him on that. So yes, my position has evolved. But I wouldn't like to see the American who, faced with 15 million abortions, isn't rethinking his or her position."

Four years later, in a debate with Governor Michael Dukakis, Bush was asked if abortion became illegal again, should women having them go to jail. "I haven't sorted out the penalties," he replied, "but I do know that I oppose abortion, and I favor adoption." He said that his position on the issue is "continuing to evolve and it's evolving in favor of life. And I had a couple of exceptions that I support — rape, incest, and the life of the mother.... I'm for the sanctity of life. And once that illegality is established, then we can come to grips with the penalty side, and of course there's got to be some penalties to enforce the law, whatever they may be."

The following day, Bush campaign chairman James Baker told the media that, after a discussion with his staff, the presidential nominee had concluded that even if abortion were outlawed, women having abortions should not be punished (these women "would more properly be considered an additional victim"), but the doctors performing them should be prosecuted.

Shortly after he was elected, however, Mr. Bush nominated as his Secretary of Health and Human Services Dr. Louis W. Sullivan, who was known to support "a woman's right to have an abortion." Sullivan had also backed Dr. Kenneth Edelin, the Boston physician convicted of manslaughter in the 1970s for killing a baby after an botched abortion, and had helped raise money for Edelin's successful appeal of his guilty verdict.

The HHS nominee headed off a brouhaha by aligning his views with those of the President-elect, stating that "my personal position is that I am opposed to abortion except in the case of rape, incest, or threat to the life of the mother."

When pro-abortion forces in the fall of 1989 attached to a

spending bill for the Departments of Education, Labor, and Health and Human Services an amendment to allow federal funding of abortion in cases of rape or incest, President Bush vetoed the bill. In a letter to Senator Robert C. Byrd (D-WV) announcing his intention to veto the legislation, Mr. Bush gave a very cogent explanation for his action:

> That such a child may have been conceived through an unconscionable act of violence makes this question difficult and indeed agonizing. It does not, however, alter the basic fact that federal funding is being sought that would compound a violent act with the taking of an unborn life. And in the absence of perfect legislation that would reconcile these difficult issues, if I have to err, I prefer to err on the side of human life.

The President's veto was upheld in the House of Representatives on October 25th and, two days later, he vetoed a budget measure for the District of Columbia that would also have permitted the use of federal funds for abortion in cases of rape and incest. The House on November 15th capitulated to Mr. Bush and declined to provide the sought-after funds.

Pro-lifers would like to think that they have an unswerving ally in the White House, but there are other indicators that make them nervous. Even though he has consistently vetoed federal money for rape and incest victims seeking abortions (they represent an estimated one percent of the 1.6 million abortions performed in the United States each year), Mr. Bush's aides hint that he would like to change his position. "The President has discussed with his advisors ways that he could move back to his pre-Ronald Reagan stance of favoring federal money for abortions in cases of rape and incest," said Maureen Dowd in the December 31, 1989 *New York Times* . In January 1990, Lee Atwater, chairman of the Republican National Committee, said that there was room in the Republican Party for people on both sides of the abortion question. "Our party is big enough to accommodate different views on plenty of issues," said Atwater. "That, my friends, is part of the growing pains of becoming a majority. And we are an umbrella party."

Gary Bauer, a foe of abortion and a former domestic policy advisor in the Reagan White House, took issue with Atwater. "If you go around saying our party is big enough for people no matter what their view on abortion, I think you signal that it's not an important issue," said Bauer. "We would not go around saying that the party is big enough for people who want to raise federal income taxes, and we would not go around saying the party is big enough for people who want to gut the defense budget."

President Bush addressed pro-life rallies in Washington by telephone in January and April, l990, and Vice President Quayle spoke in person to the huge throng at the Washington Monument on April 28, 1990. The President has also consistently opposed sending U.S. funds to the International Planned Parenthood Federation and the United Nations Fund for Population Activities because those organizations either promote abortion or support coercive population control programs.

But the *New York Times* reported in May 1990 that Bush advisors had told *Newsweek* magazine that Barbara Bush and the female members of the family all favor abortion, while the men in the family are against it. Pro-lifers hope that the President won't be swayed on this issue by his wife or the other females in the Bush clan.

AIDS and Homosexuality

The battle between pragmatism and principle also continued with regard to homosexual activists and those seeking more funds to treat victims of AIDS. Mr. Bush startled even some of his strongest boosters when he invited more than 20

homosexuals to the White House in April 1990 for the signing
of the Hate Crimes Statistics Act. That bill, which wrote
sexual orientation into law for the first time, was called a
"landmark development" by the *Washington Blade*, the
capital's homosexual weekly. Many conservatives believed
that the primary purpose of the bill was to confer legitimacy
on the homosexual lifestyle. As for the invitation itself, Robert
Bray of the National Gay and Lesbian Task Force said, "We
were stunned. No President has ever invited a group of gay and
lesbian activists to the White House."

Also stunned by the invitation was Senator William Armstrong (R-CO), who sent a strongly worded letter to the
President on April 26th. Senator Armstrong said:

> Your power to grant or withhold recognition is
> enormously influential. So it is very hard to understand
> why you would choose to exercise this power in a way
> that honors or legitimatizes those who advocate aber-
> rant behavior as a valid alternative lifestyle.
>
> Homosexuality has long been recognized as anti-
> social and destructive. Inviting such groups to the
> White House gives them a status they have never
> previously achieved and undermines the pastors,
> teachers, youth workers, and others who are trying to
> hold the line against immorality....
>
> Mr. President, what it comes down to is this: Since
> the office you hold is a "bully pulpit," it makes a huge
> difference whom you invite to share that pulpit with
> you. Such groups should never be given official rec-
> ognition by your office any more than you would give
> such status to the Ku Klux Klan or similar extremist
> groups.

Barbara Bush has also given status to these activists.
Responding in the spring of 1990 to a letter from Paulette

Goodman, president of the Federation of Parents and Friends of Lesbians and Gays, Mrs. Bush wrote: "I firmly believe that we cannot tolerate discrimination against any individuals or groups in our country." Mrs. Goodman had asked for some "kind words" to homosexuals and their families, saying that "we who have lifted the veil of ignorance ... know that our gay and lesbian children are fine, responsible, contributing members of our community. They deserve our love and support ... full human and civil rights, and the respect accorded all citizens."

In reply, Mrs. Bush said that Mrs. Goodman appeared to be a "caring parent and a compassionate citizen.... I appreciate so much ... your encouraging me to help change attitudes." It is one thing to oppose discrimination against or mistreatment of homosexuals and to sympathize with parents of children who have chosen this unnatural lifestyle. One can hate the sin while still loving the sinner. But it is quite another thing to applaud a call for "full human and civil rights" for those who have put themselves and society at risk with their immoral behavior. Yet, both President and Mrs. Bush have adopted the latter course.

On June 1, 1987, Vice President Bush spoke at the Third International Conference on AIDS in Washington and was booed when he called for wider testing of individuals at both state and federal levels to detect the AIDS virus. Referring to the booing after the speech, Bush, unaware that the microphones were picking up his words, asked Assistant HHS Secretary Robert Windom, "Who was that? Some gay group out there?" His comments were widely reported and criticized.

Nearly three years later, President Bush addressed a conference in Washington sponsored by the National Leadership Coalition on AIDS and expressed support for legislation that would prevent discrimination against disabled people, including those with AIDS. He also said that "there is only one way to deal with an individual who is sick: with dignity, compassion, care, confidentiality, and without discrimination.... We don't spurn the accident victim who didn't wear a seat belt. We don't reject the cancer patient who didn't quit smoking cigarettes. We try to love them and care for them and comfort them. We do not fire them. We don't evict them. We don't cancel their insurance."

Having compassion for those suffering from AIDS, or any other serious illness, is certainly laudable, but that's not the same as supporting laws giving homosexuals equal status with the handicapped. The militants are not looking for compassion; they're looking for approval of their perverted lifestyle. No one has been more caring and responsive to the needs of AIDS sufferers than John Cardinal O'Connor of New York, yet he has been a special target of the homosexuals. They hate him not because he lacks compassion but because he refuses to sanction their immoral behavior.

In April 1990, the Bush Administration pandered to the AIDS lobby again. It waived a policy that had previously required foreigners known to be infected with the virus to declare their illness, apply for a visa, and seek a 30-day exemption from a restriction that barred those with communicable diseases from entering the country. Under pressure from the homosexual lobby, the Administration replaced this sensible policy with one that asked no questions and granted a special 10-day visa to those wishing to attend meetings allegedly in the public interest, such as the Sixth International Conference on AIDS which was held in San Francisco in June 1990.

Senator Gordon Humphrey (R-NH) has pointed out that the Bush Administration's request for $3.46 billion for AIDS-related programs in fiscal 1991 was a billion dollars more than the amount sought for heart disease, cancer, and diabetes combined. Those three diseases, said Humphrey, "kill about one and a half million Americans each year—nearly 20 times the number of AIDS fatalities over the past 10 years.... Is this rational? Is this a logical allocation of funds among the various programs dealing with major health afflictions."

Funding for the Arts

From 1965 to 1990, the federal government spent over $4 billion funding various kinds of art, some of which probably would never have seen the light of day without this taxpayer subsidy. Although a great deal of imagination was required to view some of those works as art, it was not until 1989 and 1990 that the public's sensibilities were truly tested by Robert Mapplethorpe's photographs of homosexual acts, such as a man urinating into the mouth of another man, and children in erotic poses. Andres Serrano's depiction of a crucifix submerged in the artist's own urine was also classified as art, and Americans were outraged to learn that $45,000 in tax money had been spent to promote exhibits featuring those abominations.

In response to this outrage, Senator Jesse Helms (R-NC) led the Senate to approve restrictions on the use of federal funds to "promote, disseminate, or produce obscene or indecent materials, including but not limited to depictions of sado-masochism, homoeroticism, the exploitation of children, or individuals engaged in sex acts; or material which denigrates the objects or beliefs of the adherents of a particular religion or non-religion." The best the House of Representatives could do at the time was vote to reduce the annual $171 million appropriation for the National Endowment for the Arts (NEA) by the above-mentioned $45,000.

On March 21, 1990, NEA Chairman John E. Frohnmayer told a House subcommittee that the Bush Administration was opposed to legislation that would ban the funding of obscene art. "I and the National Endowment for the Arts oppose obscenity unequivocally," said Frohnmayer. "It is the antithesis of art. It is without a soul. It conveys no message. It degrades humanity, and it sickens me." But he said that

Congress should not pass any laws that would impose "content restrictions" on what the NEA funded.

President Bush backed his NEA chairman at a news conference, saying that "I have full confidence in John Frohnmayer." Mr. Bush said that while he was opposed to some of the NEA-funded "filth," he was "against censorship.... I don't know of anybody in the government or a government agency that should be set up to censor what you write, or what you paint, or how you express yourself."

The issue, of course, is not censorship. "The truth is," said cultural critic Hilton Kramer, "that artists in this country today enjoy a greater degree of freedom of expression than artists have enjoyed in any known civilization in the past, and to confuse the rejection of a grant application with some kind of categorical threat to freedom of expression is simply ridiculous."

The real issue is whether taxpayers should have to pay for promoting obscene and blasphemous trash. Mr. Bush is not a stupid man. Surely he understands what this debate is all about. Why, then, did he choose to side with the radical left and those who would rub the noses of the American people in this filth? The nation would have been better served had he repeated what Thomas Jefferson said in 1777: "To compel a man to furnish funds for the propagation of ideas he disbelieves and abhors is sinful and tyrannical."

There is nothing in the Constitution of the United States that gives the government the authority to finance the arts. "If Serrano wants to put a crucifix in urine and call it whatever he wants on his own time and his own money, that is fine," said the Reverend Donald Wildmon, head of the American Family Association. "If you want government money to do it, that is a whole other issue."

The way to resolve this fiasco is to do away with all appropriations for the arts. "Censorship is not the solution," said Representative Dana Rohrabacher (R-CA). "The answer is getting the government out of the arts."

Minimum Wage Increases

In 1988, George Bush ran for President on a platform that said: "We are the party of real social progress.... So we will remove disincentives that keep the less fortunate out of the productive economy.... As an alternative to inflationary and job-destroying increases in the minimum wage, we will work to boost the incomes of the working poor through the Earned Income Tax Credit, especially for earners who support children. This will mean higher take-home pay for millions of working families."

Numerous economic studies have shown that hikes in the minimum wage actually put people out of work. When the government orders an increase in hourly wages, employers whose businesses are just barely making a profit are forced to lay off workers in order to survive. Yet Mr. Bush in November 1989 signed into law a bill increasing the minimum wage from $3.35 to $4.25 an hour by April 1991. "I have called for an increase in the minimum wage that would protect jobs and put more money into the pockets of our workers," he said at the signing ceremony. "In my view, this bill does exactly that. I'm pleased to sign it. It offers the promise of better wages for the working men and women and gives incentive to create new jobs for our young people."

What the President's own party had called a "job-destroying" factor in 1988 had somehow become a job-protecting instrument in 1989! The pragmatic Mr. Bush could make that switch without batting an eye. And, as usual, his switch ended up favoring the liberal-leftist point of view.

Tax Increases

If there is one pledge for which George Bush is famous, it was his unequivocal statement at the Republican National Convention on August 18, 1988: "The Congress will push me to raise taxes, and I'll say no, and they'll push, and I'll say no, and they'll push again, and I'll say to them, 'Read my lips: No new taxes.' " In *Leadership on the Issues*, a collection of his statements, Mr. Bush explained his opposition to new taxes:

> In the past several years, tax increases have been used to feed congressional spending, not for true deficit reduction. This should be a warning to all future Presidents against tax hikes. Unless you can control Congress' spending, increased revenues will go to increased spending.
>
> The most important action we need to take on the budget deficit is to hold the line on taxing and spending. Raising taxes would only hurt the tremendous economic recovery we have had in our Administration.

On January 29, 1990, President Bush proposed a $1.23 trillion budget for fiscal 1991, with an estimated deficit of $63.1 billion. The budget included $15.7 billion in new taxes! These were not income taxes but telephone excise taxes, airline ticket taxes, stock transaction taxes, and other devices to separate the American people from their money in order to finance the voracious monster of gargantuan government. Mr. Bush had not taken very long to break his pledge of "no new taxes."

In the spring of 1990, rumors began emanating from the White House that Mr. Bush was wavering even more on his no-tax pledge. Presidential Press Secretary Marlin Fitzwater, reporting on May 7th about a meeting the previous night between the President and congressional leaders, said: "What they did agree to last night was that they would not get involved in discussions about taxation or specific issues, but rather to stick to the phrase 'no preconditions' and begin an open debate that is unfettered with conclusions about positions taken in the past."

Senator Alan Simpson (R-WY), who attended the meeting, said that "all sorts of things" were discussed in the presence of Mr. Bush — "value added taxes, additional user fees, taxes on booze and cigarettes, a national lottery, a one-cent national sales tax." Thus does the Bush Administration "at last define itself," said Patrick Buchanan. "There is no conservative party in Washington now, just two government parties that disagree on which programs to fund, what taxes to raise."

The charade came to an end on June 26, 1990, when President Bush said that any solution to the deficit problem would have to include "tax revenue increases." At a news conference three days later, Mr. Bush said that he was "not violating or getting away from my fundamental conviction on taxes, anything of that nature. Not in the least. But ... we've got a very important national problem, and I think the President owes the people his judgment at the moment he has to address that problem." On September 30th, he completed his reversal by striking a budget deal with congressional negotiators that called for $134 billion in new taxes and user fees.

Mr. Bush's flip-flop on his "Read my lips: No new taxes" promise calls to mind the comedian who said, "You can tell when a politician is lying if his lips are moving." The joke, however, is on the American people.

Terrorism

His year at the helm of the CIA and his three years as chairman of the Vice President's Task Force on Combatting Terrorism have given Mr. Bush considerable information on the problem of terrorism. He has spoken out on the subject many times and, in November 1988, released a report from his Task Force in which he said that, first, "the United States will be firm with terrorists," second, "we will apply pressure to states which sponsor terrorism," and third, "we will bring terrorists to justice." His record in that regard is not very good.

For one thing, Mr. Bush has not always been candid about those behind international terrorism. In an introductory letter that he wrote for the 1988 report on *Terrorist Group Profiles,* the then-Vice President said that "governments sponsoring terrorism include North Korea, Iran, Libya, Syria, and South Yemen." He did not mention the Soviet Union which had long been the principal sponsor of worldwide terrorist activity.

Stark evidence supporting this indictment of the USSR was spelled out in "The Tel Aviv Declaration," a statement that came out of a conference on state terrorism held in Israel in January 1986. The meeting was attended by 60 prominent senior statesmen (active and retired), military officers, and national security specialists from a dozen countries. The following is excerpted from the full statement carried in the February 9, 1986 edition of the *New York Times* :

> But neither Mr. Reagan nor any of the leaders of the West can have any illusions about the role of the Soviet Union in fostering and stimulating, sponsoring and training, funding and arming terrorist groups and governments around the world. This is not to suggest that the Soviets push the buttons and that their hand is always, directly or indirectly, in play. None of us subscribe to that kind of oversimplification. But where they do not initiate it, they encourage it. Where they have not organized it, they exploit it....
>
> A "Radical Entente" presently spearheaded by five militant states (Syria, Libya, Iran, North Korea, and Cuba) is making coordinated efforts — by themselves and with others — to undermine the power and influence of the United States and its allies. Here the well-documented role of the Soviet Union is to provide the professional infrastructure of terrorism, including money, arms, explosives, recruitment and training, passports, infiltration and escape routes, transport, communications, safe havens, control officers, and more. Taken together, these constitute an elaborate

international network of support systems for terrorists.

George Bush was certainly aware of this information when he wrote his introduction to *Terrorist Group Profiles*, so why did he fail to mention the Soviet Union? Was he afraid of showing the true character of the regime headed by his friend Mikhail Gorbachev? If the American people knew of the Kremlin's massive role in the terror conspiracy that has taken the lives of so many American citizens, would they be so agreeable to bailing out Gorbachev and salvaging perestroika?

In that same introductory letter, Mr. Bush noted the terror campaign being waged against Pakistan "by agents of the Afghan intelligence service known as WAD. The WAD is Soviet trained and organized. The terrorist campaign is designed to deter the government of Pakistan from aiding resistance fighters in Afghanistan." This letter was dated November 1988, three months after Soviet-backed terrorists blew up a plane whose victims included not only Pakistani President Zia and nearly 30 of his top aides and army officers, but also U.S. Ambassador Arnold L. Raphael and Brigadier General Herbert M. Wassom, the chief American military attache in Pakistan. Yet, Vice President Bush said not a word about this brutal atrocity. Why?

It is easy to talk tough about terrorism; it is quite another thing to do something about it. "The key is to punish severely those states that provide safe haven and logistical support to terrorist groups," said anti-terrorism expert Robert Kupperman in a book entitled *Final Warning*, written with Jeff Kamen. "Without secure bases, arms, and money, terrorist groups are largely ineffective. The United States and its allies must move quickly. If not, terrorism will metastasize beyond control."

But what has the Bush Administration done to deal effectively with this threat? When an American military officer was killed in Panama in December 1989, President Bush said that nobody gets away with killing Americans. But terrorists had already gotten away with killing more than 40 Americans on Pan American Flight 103 over Scotland in December 1988, and with hanging a U.S. Marine officer in Lebanon in July 1989 and showing him on videotape swinging from a rope. They have also gotten away with killing at least nine American military personnel in the Philippines since 1987.

We know who the major terrorist criminals are and who is providing them with the infrastructure of terror. If we are serious about stopping terrorism, we must put the Qaddafis, Assads, and Arafats out of business, along with the organizations they support and direct. We must warn their suppliers, whether they be the Soviet Union, Soviet client states, or our supposed "allies" in Western Europe, to stop aiding those regimes and trading with them.

But the Bush Administration has set a poor example. On May 30, 1990, less than a week after a State Department official had told Congress that Yasir Arafat's Palestine Liberation Organization (PLO) had kept its December 1988 promise not to engage in terrorism, the Israelis apprehended six boatloads of PLO terrorists heading for the crowded beaches of Tel Aviv with grenade launchers and machine guns. The leader of the abortive raid was Abul Abbas, hijacker of the *Achille Lauro* cruise ship and a member of the PLO Executive Committee.

But it was another three weeks before President Bush finally suspended talks with the PLO that had been going on for 18 months. He explained that he had given the PLO "ample time" to condemn the thwarted terrorist strike against Israel and punish those responsible, but the terrorist faction had failed to do so. Mr. Bush did not explain why his Administration had been negotiating at all with the PLO since its members have such total disregard for innocent human life.

Also belying President Bush's alleged opposition to terrorism was his effusive welcome at the White House for South African terrorist Nelson Mandela on June 25, 1990. (For details on Mandela's background, see Chapter 5.) This was the same Mandela who had been named the latest winner of the Lenin Peace Prize just before arriving in the United States; who had declared his admiration for Fidel Castro, Yasir Arafat, and Muammar Qaddafi on the June 21st ABC *Nightline* program; and who had paid tribute that same day to four Puerto Rican terrorists (he called them "comrades") who had shot five Congressman in a 1954 attack within the U.S. House of Representatives.

But President Bush treated this criminal terrorist like a head of state, honoring him with a ceremony on the White House lawn, a luncheon, and three hours of talks. Mr. Bush publicly asked Mandela to "renounce violence and repression" but was rebuffed by the African National Congress (ANC) leader, who said that when a government intensifies its oppression, "the people have no alternative but to resort to violence."

Mandela even chastised the President by saying that Mr. Bush's remarks about nonviolence were "due to the fact he has not as yet got a proper briefing from us." He said he would urge the President "not to do anything without full consultation with the ANC in regard to any initiative which he might propose to take in order to help the peace process in the country." Instead of being insulted by these belittling remarks, Mr. Bush responded by thanking Mandela for his comments and saying, "Good statement. No notes. It's wonderful."

Traveling through the United States just ahead of Mandela in June 1990 was Tamsanqa Linda, the black former mayor of Ibhayi township, a municipality of over 400,000 black South Africans. The courageous Mayor Linda had been targeted for assassination by the ANC, and his home and the homes of relatives and friends had been firebombed by ANC terrorist squads because of his unyielding opposition to the ANC and the South African Communist Party.

In an interview with *The New American*, Linda said that he came to the United States to tell the American people the truth about Mandela "and the movement he represents. We are fighting for our lives and our freedom in South Africa but, contrary to what you may hear, it is not the government that is the main threat to black people, but Mandela and his communist terrorist ANC." The mayor, who was not invited to the White House, said that

> ... we cannot understand why your government and others in the West seem determined to force on us the same Marxist system that has caused such widespread death, destruction, and misery throughout southern Africa. We have the potential to be a peaceful, productive, prosperous, democratic, multiracial country much like yours, and that is what we want. We need the whites, and they need us. The same for the Indians and coloreds. It is only a small minority of both black and white extremists who are thwarting progress. We are asking you, the American people, not to allow your government to undermine our hopes and aspirations for a peaceful and free South Africa.

What is needed to win the war against terrorism, said Benjamin Netanyahu, former Israeli Ambassador to the United Nations and author of the book *Terrorism: How the West Can Win*, is political courage from government leaders, particularly in the United States. He said that "only a determined leadership can make the West overcome the greed, cowardice, and moral confusion that foster terrorism. It can come only from the United States, which alone has the capacity to align the West's resistance, alone can credibly threaten the offenders, and alone can compel neutrals to shed their neutrality. The more the United States resorts to action, like punishing terrorists and their backers, the greater the number of states that will join the American effort to combat terrorism."

When will President Bush demonstrate this kind of political courage and determined leadership and back up his promises with deeds?

Senator Bill Armstrong
protested homosexual
presence at a
White House function.

Richard Darman typifies
the leftwing activism of
the Bush Administration.

A.P./Wide World Photos

Dr. Louis Sullivan won the
Human Services post after
his switch on abortion.

Sen. Gordon Humphrey
said Mr. Bush went
overboard on AIDS-
related budget.

Chapter 3
The Collectivist

In chasing votes at any cost, Mr. Bush is doing something more than letting down his own natural constituency. He is abetting the erosion of principles we had once thought transcended any narrow interest: property rights, limited government, and the indispensable stipulation that, in any prosecution, the burden of proof is on the accuser, not the defendant.

— Editorial in *National Review*,
June 11, 1990

The Constitution of the United States is a blueprint for limited government. The men who wrote and ratified that document knew that big government leads to tyranny, so they set out to limit the government, not the people. They gave the federal government only certain specified powers, chiefly to protect our God-given rights to life, liberty, and property, and left all other powers to the states or to the people. The system worked well for about 150 years and the freedoms it guaranteed to the people transformed America into one of the greatest and most prosperous nations in history.

Over the past half-century, however, the Constitution has been ignored by Republican and Democratic administrations alike, and the principles that made America great have been virtually discarded. A people that once believed in the least government possible now thinks the federal government has a duty to solve all problems, address all needs, and redistribute the wealth by taking from some in order to give to others. Many Americans today seem never to have learned that a government big enough to give you everything you want is big enough to take away everything you have.

Whether the opposite of true Americanism is called collectivism or socialism, it will be characterized by economic control of the people by the state through state management of the means of production and distribution (natural resources, factories, farms, machinery, tools, money, transportation, and communications). It can be totalitarian socialism as in the Soviet Union, or democratic socialism as in Britain (and, increasingly, in the United States), but control by the state is the fundamental characteristic.

The certain fruits of economic control are scarcity and hardship. Where collectivism and socialism reign, incentive to work and produce dies. No matter how diligent you are, how well you use your God-given talents, or how inventive or creative you might be, whatever your labor and energy produce will be taken away from you by the omnipotent state, either physically or through regulation and taxation. At the same time, those who perform poorly or produce nothing at all will become wards of the state. Human nature being what it is, many people will see little sense in working hard for something that they cannot keep, or working at all if the government will take care of them.

How socialistic is the United States? "The U.S. is now 45 percent socialist," said free-market economist Milton Friedman in an Op-Ed piece for the *New York Times* on the last day of 1989. He arrived at that figure by calculating that "spending by government currently amounts to about 45 percent of national income. By that test, government owns 45 percent of the means of production that produce the national income."

The loss of freedom is even worse than that, said Friedman, when one considers that "government exercises extensive direct control over how the means of production may be used: It prohibits certain uses (to deliver first class mail, to sell some drugs at all, to sell others without prescription, etc.); it controls other uses through laws governing wages, hours, and working conditions, rent control, and in other ways."

As the government has expanded its control over more and more facets of American life, said Friedman, "we have ended up performing essential governmental functions far less well than is not only possible but than was attained earlier. In a poorer and less socialist era, we produced a nationwide network of roads and bridges and subway systems that were the envy of the world. Today we are unable even to maintain them."

Does this deteriorating situation disturb the populace and lead to calls for less government? On the contrary, said Friedman, the loudest complaints are that "government should be doing more; government is strapped for funds; taxes should be raised; more regulations should be imposed; build more prisons to house more criminals created by socialist legislation. Child care? Program trading? Earthquakes? Pass a law. And every law comes with a price tag and is cited as a reason for higher taxes."

Sound familiar? It should; it's all you hear in the halls of Congress these days. And the same sounds are coming from the White House. Remember George Bush's State of the Union address on January 31, 1990? He called on Congress to "work together to do the will of the people. Clean air. Child care. The excellence in education bill. Crime and drugs. It's time to act. The farm bill. Transportation policy. Product liability reform. Enterprise zones. It's time to act together." You name it, President Bush has a federal government plan to do something about it.

This is the same George Bush who said in his 1987 autobiography: "I believe, as did Jefferson and Lincoln, that the sole purpose of government is to do for people what they can't do for themselves." And in his 1988 acceptance speech at the GOP convention, the President-to-be said that an occupant of the White House "must see to it that government intrudes as little as possible in the lives of the people." Mr. Bush has not explained how a government that does for people those things they allegedly cannot do for themselves can at the same time intrude as little as possible in their lives.

It was the same George Bush who promised in 1980 that a Republican Administration would get "the professional regulators off the backs of American industry," who headed President Reagan's Task Force on Regulatory Relief and was praised by Mr. Reagan in 1984 for having "reduced the growth of federal regulations by more than 25 percent," and who said in his autobiography that, as Vice President, "I was able to follow through on one of our key 1980 campaign pledges — to cut red tape and get the federal government off the backs of the American people."

But this was also the George Bush who, in his first economic report to Congress in 1990, called for greater federal involvement in child care, education, and environmental protection. "In some cases," Mr. Bush said, "well-designed regulation can serve the public interest." Consider some of the "well-designed regulation" supported by President Bush and see how well it serves the public interest.

Clean Air Legislation

In June 1989, President Bush unveiled a clean air plan that he said would cut acid rain by 50 percent, reduce smog in 78 cities, and curb the release of airborne toxic chemicals by industry by 75 to 90 percent. "We've seen enough of this stalemate," he said. "It's time to clear the air." Mr. Bush didn't go far enough with his plan, said Democratic leaders in Congress, so a "compromise" proposal was worked out, one whose cost, according to unnamed White House officials, would be from $12 billion to as much as $24 billion above what the President said would be his "veto-line" target of $22 billion.

What kind of a compromise is it when one party (Mr. Bush) agrees to accept a plan that will cost at least 50 percent more than he said he would accept? Furthermore, said economic columnist Warren Brookes at that time, the Clean Air Act would impose a huge regulatory burden on American industry even though U.S. anti-pollution spending was already $85 billion a year, "double that of the entire 12-nation European Community ... and four times the equivalent per capita level of Great Britain."

Brookes said that reduced health risks would be virtually nonexistent and that, in every area, "the costs infinitely outweigh either health or environmental benefits." He also charged that supporters of the Clean Air Act were "going for some of the most idiotic programs I've ever seen and legislating a new frame of reference that's going to give the EPA life-and-death control over every plant in this country."

Environmental Hysteria

The Clean Air Act is only one phase of the drive for an all-powerful central government. Huge and expensive bureaucracies are being created in response to a propaganda barrage about protecting the environment and saving us from acid rain, the "greenhouse" effect, ozone depletion, deforestation, overpopulation, and pollution of the air and water. Hysterical claims and phony statistics are frightening otherwise sensible people into believing that doomsday is fast approaching and only a greatly expanded federal government can preserve our civilization.

A President who is a true leader would use his powerful office to defuse these misleading and dangerous exaggerations. Instead, Mr. Bush signed a formal proclamation designating April 22, 1990 as "Earth Day '90," and he added his own invitation for an "international alliance" to deal with unproven environmental threats.

The President chose not to rely on writers Warren Brookes

and Robert W. Lee, economists Jacqueline Kasun and Hans Sennholz, and scientist Dr. Petr Beckmann, all of whom, along with growing numbers of colleagues, have convincingly demonstrated that most of the environmentalists' claims are without scientific foundation. Sadly for the future of a free America, the mass media continue to sound numerous false alarms. Even more sadly, the President joins in.

The publicity generated by the media for Earth Day '90 was phenomenal. The *Washington Post* alone ran 56 stories about the Earth Day celebration in the nation's capital, which was attended by approximately 125,000 persons. In contrast, the *Post* ran only two stories on the Rally for Life '90 a week later that attracted upwards of 500,000 persons demanding an end to abortion.

Another chilling example of media-driven hysteria was the Great Alar Scare of 1989. Alar is a substance sprayed on apple blossoms to enhance the appearance of the apples and keep them from falling off the trees. But Ed Bradley, relying on a report by an environmental lobby known as the Natural Resources Defense Council, charged in a February 26, 1989 segment of the CBS program *60 Minutes* that Alar was the "most potent cancer-causing agent in our food supply." The report was based on a long-discredited 1977 study in which rats were fed 48 times their maximum tolerable dosage of Alar, killing them prematurely.

Extensive animal studies since then have shown that Alar is not a carcinogen in mice or rats and poses no threat of causing cancer in humans. "Nonetheless," reported Robert W. Lee, "the Great Alar Scare cost apple growers an estimated $100 million, generated undue fear and stress among countless parents and children, and stands as yet another example of what can be accomplished when special interests, the media, and federal regulatory agencies conspire in wildly exaggerating an issue to wreck a private industry and expand government power."

Shortly after he was elected President, George Bush said, "I am an environmentalist." Now there is nothing wrong with being reasonably concerned about protecting the environment. All of us want to live in a society that is relatively free of pollution, and in an atmosphere where we are able to enjoy the beautiful scenic wonders of America. What we don't want is to be forced to trade our property rights, our freedom to travel, and our right to be economically self-sufficient for a return to the pristine environment that existed before the first humans arrived. The earth and the environment exist to be used responsibly, not set on a pedestal and worshipped.

According to a 1989 study by the Harvard Energy and Environmental Policy Center, existing government legislation is slowing down the growth of the U.S. economy. "The cost of environmental regulation is a long-run reduction of 2.59 percent in the level of the U.S. gross national product," said the authors of the study, Dale W. Jorgenson and Peter J. Wilcoxen. That is a staggering slice of America's productivity, and the situation can only grow worse as more stringent environmental controls are imposed on the American people. President Bush has talked about striking a balance between economic growth and environmental preservation, but the latter seems to be prevailing over the former.

On July 6, 1989, Mr. Bush signed into law the Natural Gas Wellhead Decontrol Act and said the "clear message" of the act was that "the best way to deal with our energy problems and serve the American people is to let our market economy work." A few weeks later, however, he directed his Secretary of Energy "to take the lead in developing a comprehensive, national energy strategy…. Our task, our bipartisan task, is to build the national consensus necessary to support this strategy and to make this strategy a living and dynamic document responsive to new knowledge and new ideas and to global, environmental, and international changes."

The Department of Energy is a perfect example of what

happens when energy supplies are determined by bureaucrats instead of the market. Created in 1977, the department spends billions of dollars each year but has never produced a drop of oil, a lump of coal, or a cubic foot of natural gas. What it has done is inhibit geologists, miners, engineers, drillers, and others from solving America's energy needs by burying them under a mountain of regulations, controls, and taxes. During the 1973-1974 energy crisis, which was a crisis of distribution and not supply, America was importing aproximately one-third of its oil. By 1990, after an explosion of the federal presence in the energy field, our nation was importing 50 percent of its oil!

President Bush helped to exacerbate that situation in June 1990 by suspending for up to 10 years the sale of oil leases off the coasts of New England, Florida, Washington, Oregon, and California. "The development of oil and gas on the outer continental shelf should occur in an environmentally sound manner," the President said in announcing the moratorium.

The Mobil oil company found Mr. Bush's action hard to understand. In a paid ad that appeared in the July 19, 1990 *New York Times*, Mobil said:

> We've noted that offshore drilling is eminently safe; some five billion barrels of oil were produced in U.S. waters during the last 17 years, and about 900 barrels were spilled during blowouts at production wells. During that time, spills from blowouts at exploratory wells totaled zero.
>
> We've also pointed out many times that as U.S. oil production dwindles, this nation will have to import more oil, and that imported oil reaches our shores by tanker. So in reaction to recent tanker spills, we seem to have adopted a no-drill policy that's certain to increase the amount of tanker traffic. If there's any logic at work here, it escapes us.

Cabinet Status for EPA

In another demonstration of his penchant for collectivism, President Bush on January 24, 1990, proposed making the Environmental Protection Agency a Cabinet department. "The environmental challenges that face America and the world are so important that they must be addressed from the highest level of our government," the President said at a news conference. "With so many difficult decisions ahead, I'll need Bill Reilly's counsel. I'll need him sitting at my side in the Cabinet, and I'm pleased to endorse the elevation of the EPA to Cabinet status by creating a Department of the Environment."

If Mr. Bush needs EPA chief William Reilly at his side, couldn't he just invite him to a Cabinet meeting when environmental issues were on the agenda, rather than create a brand new Cabinet department with all the added expense and bureaucracy? But that would indicate a desire to keep government from expanding even further into the lives of people, and such a desire does not seem to be in the mind of the President.

Ever since President Nixon illegitimately conceived the EPA by executive order in 1970, the agency has run roughshod over people and industry. "If the EPA's conception of its mission is permitted to stand," said New York University's Irving Kristol in 1974, "it will be the single most powerful branch of government, having far greater control over our individual lives than Congress, or the executive, or state and local government." These powers will only be enhanced by moving the EPA into the Cabinet.

The environmental extremists had gotten a present from Mr. Bush when he named one of their own, William K. Reilly of the Conservation Foundation, as head of EPA. Reilly was the first "Green" chosen to run the EPA since Russell Train in the Ford Administration. He said that he had received from President Bush "a program that adds 50 percent or maybe more to what the country lays out on pollution control every year. And, by heaven, that is a strong measure of presidential commitment."

In "Greening the White House," an article that appeared in the August 13, 1989 *New York Times Magazine*, environmentalist Trip Gabriel boasted that "Reilly has had this President's ear like no other chief in the agency's 19 years." Gabriel offered the following assessment of Mr. Bush's commitment to the environment:

> As Vice President, George Bush was a leader of the anti-regulatory assault, earning a D-rating for his record from the League of Conservation Voters. This raises an intriguing issue: In declaring himself an environmentalist, appointing Reilly and heeding his advice, has Bush shown that he is secretly a Green? Or has he mostly made a political decision to steal the environmental issue from the Democrats? Either way, the environment may reap the benefits.

What is also true is that, either way, big government will grow bigger, and the freedoms of the people will be diminished.

Earth Day '90

Another boost for the environmental cause was President Bush's proclamation of April 22, 1990, as "Earth Day '90" in order to "heighten public awareness of the need for active participation in the protection of the environment and to promote the formation of an international alliance that responds to global environmental concerns." Notice that national concerns have been expanded beyond the borders of the United States, something which those promoting a new world order have been emphasizing for some time. For example, Columbia University Professor Richard N. Gardner used the Spring 1988 issue of *Foreign Affairs*, the journal of the

Council on Foreign Relations, to recommend the use of environmental concerns as a stepping-stone to entangling America in internationalism.

This is the same Richard Gardner who, in the April 1974 issue of *Foreign Affairs* ("The Hard Road to World Order"), said that it would be difficult to get America to make a single leap into a world government via the United Nations. What he suggested instead was "an end run around national sovereignty, eroding it piece by piece." The American people could not be expected to relinquish control over their own national affairs all at once, but they might be persuaded to give up bits of their sovereignty and freedom through membership in various international organizations and alliances.

And what better way to motivate American citizens to take such disastrous steps than to frighten them with exaggerated scenarios about environmental catastrophes. "Environmental strains that transcend national borders are already beginning to break down the sacred boundaries of national sovereignty," said an approving Jessica Tuchman Mathews, vice president of the World Resources Institute, in the Spring 1989 issue of *Foreign Affairs.*

British musician Billy Bragg echoed the feelings of at least some of the Earth Day '90 participants in Washington when he sang the communist "Internationale" on the steps of the Capitol and declared, "We must reject capitalism. We must commit to the ideal of collectivism." Most of the speakers and organizers of the demonstration, said *Human Events*, "came from the portside of the ideological spectrum, preaching collectivism, the value of a no-growth society, disarmament, and the pagan notion that human beings have no more rights than animals and plants. Some also urged direct action, including sabotage and civil disobedience, against the supposed evils of corporate America."

According to syndicated columnist Warren Brookes, environmentalists are out of touch with reality if they think they can eliminate all risk from daily living. "In fact," he noted, "there's only one state of being with zero risk: death. And that's true in the economic world as well as the physical one. All of life is risk." Referring to the alleged dangers of global warming, Brookes said that studies by two top scientists have shown that there was no net rise in temperature in the Northern Hemisphere over the period from 1935 to 1990. "So we have a non-story here," Brookes told *Insight* magazine. "But by this time, there are all these international conferences on global warming and all this fundraising and all this bureaucracy that's been created. Don't tell them that there's no global warming because that means they have no jobs."

Back in 1973, when Congress was debating a federal land-use bill, Republican Senator Carl Curtis of Nebraska vigorously opposed the legislation. "Of course we want wise use of our resources in this country," he said, "but the part I challenge is this: I challenge the notion that government always knows best, and I specifically challenge the notion that the federal government always knows best. The federal government with its red tape, its bureaucracy, its great power, its ability to pour out billions of dollars in grants to get states and individuals to surrender their rights, is a mighty powerful institution. Yet, it is not always right."

Senator Curtis conceded that "some decisions have to be made and some authority has to be vested in order to curb the individual who has a total disregard for the rights of others, but let that power reside in the states and the localities.... American history is replete with evidence that individuals, collectively, make wiser judgments than governments. Individuals are not always right, but their mistakes are not so enormous."

The attitude expressed by Senator Curtis in 1973 is precisely what enabled our nation to grow and prosper. But if George Bush and others are successful in promoting an entirely new attitude of surrendering individual rights to the power of the federal government, America will wither and die.

The Education President

Still another area where the federal government has become harmfully dominant is the field of education. The word "education" does not appear in the United States Constitution, which means, according to the Tenth Amendment, that this entire field is supposed to be left to the states or to the people themselves. That is also common sense. Who knows better the educational needs of the children in a particular town or school district — the parents and people of that locality or some bureaucrat in Washington? Yet a huge educational establishment has been created by the federal government, and the quality of education has declined sharply as federal involvement has increased.

After promising in the 1988 election campaign to become known as "the education President," George Bush asked Congress in April 1989 for $441 million to promote academic excellence. This was on top of the $21.9 billion education budget he had submitted to Congress just two months earlier. In September 1989, the President met with the nation's governors in Charlottesville, Virginia, to find ways to improve schools. They issued a joint statement saying that "the time had come, for the first time in U.S. history, to establish clear national performance goals. This agreement represents the first step in a long-term commitment to reorient the education system and to marshal widespread support for the needed reforms."

The conferees called for parental choice of schools for their children, school management that allowed teachers and principals greater control over curriculum and budgets, alternative certification of teachers, and incentive payments for schools and teachers that raise performance levels. Although all of those recommendations could be implemented without the federal government's involvement, no one called for getting the federal government out of education.

In July 1990, the Department of Education sent an antidrug curriculum to more than 120,000 school administrators across the country. Entitled "Learning to Live Drug Free," the detailed program covered kindergarten through grade 12 and was designed to provide children with information on the social, economic, and health effects of drug abuse, said Secretary of Education Lauro F. Cavazos. He said students would learn that "drug use is part of a culture of pain and potential violence that harms both individuals and society as a whole. And they learn that they can help change this culture through their own behavior."

This marked the first time that the Department of Education had offered a curriculum model to all the nation's schools. Drugs was the topic this time, but next time it might be sex education, then history, then who knows what else? The point is, federal involvement in education is unconstitutional and federal offering (more like mandating since few if any schools would say no to the goose who provides the golden eggs) of curriculum models is another step toward a socialist America.

The federal government is now into areas where it was never supposed to be and George Bush, who swore a solemn oath to "preserve, protect, and defend the Constitution of the United States," is now promoting and supporting all kinds of unconstitutional programs and policies.

Milton Friedman has said
the United States is more
than 45 percent socialist.

Richard Gardner would
use environmentalism
to achieve world order.

Petr Beckmann has shown
environmentalist claims to
be scientifically false.

President Bush suspended
the sale of offshore oil
leases for up to ten years.

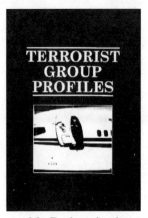

Mr. Bush omitted
evidence of Soviet
terrorism from this report.

Senator Carl Curtis
long ago opposed more
power for the federal
government.

EPA chief William Reilly
has the President's ear on
environmental issues.

Lauro Cavazos heads up
the unconstitutional
Education Department.

Chapter 4
The Internationalist

George Bush, in fact, has been a dues-paying member of the Establishment, if it is succinctly defined as the Council on Foreign Relations and the Trilateral Commission.

— Sidney Blumenthal in the
Washington Post, February 10, 1988

The word "Establishment," according to the American Heritage Dictionary, means "an exclusive group of powerful people who rule a government or society by means of private agreements and decisions." Anyone referring to the "American Establishment" must consider the following definition given by Edith Kermit Roosevelt in a syndicated column in 1961:

The word "Establishment" is a general term for the power elite in international finance, business, the professions and government, largely from the northeast, who wield most of the power regardless of who is in the White House. Most people are unaware of the existence of this "legitimate Mafia." Yet the power of the Establishment makes itself felt from the professor who seeks a foundation grant, to the candidate for a Cabinet post or State Department job. It affects the nation's policies in almost every area.

And if you want to express the notion of the Establishment even more succinctly, as Sidney Blumenthal suggested, then you must specify the Trilateral Commission and the Council on Foreign Relations, those quintessential twin peaks of elitist internationalism whose members hope to bring into existence, and preside over, a new world order. George Bush had been a member of both groups prior to the 1980 campaign and, as of 1990, was carried on the membership roster of the Trilateral Commission as a "Former Member in Public Service."

The Trilateral Commission

During his campaign for the Republican presidential nomination in 1980, Mr. Bush ran into some flak in New Hampshire and Florida about his connections with the Trilateral Commission (TC). Formed by banker David Rockefeller in 1973, the Commission set out to bring together leading internationalists from the United States, Western Europe, and Japan for the purpose of linking the three regions "in their economic relations, their political and defense relations, their relations with developing countries, and their relations with communist countries." The ultimate goal of the group was to create a world government.

One of the approximately 100 Trilateralists from the United States was Jimmy Carter, who had been invited to join by Rockefeller in 1973 while Mr. Carter was still Governor of Georgia. He later said that his Trilateral membership had "provided me with a splendid learning opportunity, and many of the members have helped me in my study of foreign affairs."

After being elected President in 1976, Mr. Carter named a number of Trilateralists to top posts in his Administration, including Cyrus Vance as Secretary of State, Harold Brown as Secretary of Defense, W. Michael Blumenthal as Secretary of the Treasury, and Zbigniew Brzezinski as his national security advisor. Each of these men was also a member of Rockefeller's other internationalist organization, the Council on Foreign Relations (CFR). President Carter, whose Vice President, Walter Mondale, was a TC member, also appointed TC and CFR member Paul Volcker as chairman of the Federal Reserve Board.

By 1979, George Bush had resigned from the TC and the CFR as his campaign was cranking up, apparently to avoid the stigma of being involved with groups pursuing a one-world agenda. He mentioned both organizations in a footnote in his 1987 autobiography *Looking Forward*, saying only that he had in 1980 run into "some of the same political types on the campaign trail" as in 1964 but, by this time, "they'd uncovered an international conspiracy even more sinister than the Council on Foreign Relations — the Trilateral Commission, a group that President Reagan received at the White House in 1981."

Mr. Bush can use all the sarcasm he wants, and give the impression that the TC can't be bad or President Reagan would never have invited its members to the White House, but the fact remains that this group seeks to replace the American system of checks and balances and limits on the power of the federal government with a monolithic control of the nation's power structures. This would mean the end of the spiritual, political, and economic freedom that has made America a beacon of hope to a world largely deprived of liberty.

"In my view," said former Senator Barry Goldwater in his 1979 book *With No Apologies*, "the Trilateral Commission represents a skillful, coordinated effort to seize control and consolidate the four centers of power — political, monetary, intellectual, and ecclesiastical. All this is to be done in the interests of creating a more peaceful, more productive world community." He cited the final paragraph of a 1975 Trilateral report, which said that "close Trilateral cooperation in keeping the peace, in managing the world economy, in fostering economic redevelopment, and alleviating world poverty will improve the chances of a smooth and peaceful evolution of the global system." Goldwater then concluded:

> What the Trilaterals truly intend is the creation of a worldwide economic power superior to the political governments of the nation-states involved. They believe the abundant materialism they propose to create will overwhelm existing differences. As managers and creators of the system they will rule the future.

It is easy to see why, during a presidential campaign when he was seeking conservative support, George Bush might not want his name connected to a group promoting this kind of sovereignty-compromising globalism. When asked about his Trilateral affiliation in 1980, he responded, "Clearly, I would never have belonged to any organization that had devious designs or favored one-world government." It is also easy to see why some Florida conservatives got under his skin with a newspaper ad whose theme was: "The same people who gave you Jimmy Carter want now to give you George Bush."

Mike Thompson, chairman of the Florida Conservative Union and author of the ad, said in an interview at the time that he was concerned about "the extremely lopsided representation of 15 of the 75 Trilateral Commission members in George Bush's campaign as contributors and workers. I have no quarrel with a legitimate liberal, but Bush is trying to portray himself as a conservative."

The Council on Foreign Relations

The ad also mentioned the Council on Foreign Relations, which Bush had joined in 1971 and served as a director before leaving in 1979. It quoted from a *Newsweek* article in 1977, which said: "Since the end of World War II, U.S. foreign policy has been dominated largely by a circle of influential men who belong to New York's Council on Foreign Relations. From Franklin D. Roosevelt to Jimmy Carter, every President has recruited Council luminaries — its membership roll is a Who's Who of the Eastern Establishment elite — for high-level diplomatic trouble-shooting missions or for top jobs in his administration. But the Council is not universally admired."

The CFR is indeed not universally admired. Who would admire an organization devoted to creating a one-world socialist system and making the United States an official part of it, except those who agreed with that plan? As expected, CFR members and defenders vigorously deny any such goal for the organization, but articles since 1922 in its own house organ, *Foreign Affairs*, contradict the denials. As do former members of the CFR and those who have made extensive studies of the group's history.

Take, for instance, Rear Admiral Chester Ward, former Judge Advocate General of the U.S. Navy and a member of the Council for 16 years. In *Kissinger on the Couch*, a 1975 book he co-authored with Phyllis Schlafly, Admiral Ward said he had reached the conclusion that the purpose of the CFR was to promote "submergence of U.S. sovereignty and national independence into an all-powerful one-world government." He declared that "this lust to surrender the sovereignty and independence of the United States is pervasive throughout most of the membership, and particularly in the leadership of the several divergent cliques that make up what is actually a polycentric organization."

One of the most devastating critiques of the CFR is *The Shadows of Power*, a 1988 book by James Perloff. After years of research that included examining every issue of *Foreign Affairs* since it began publication in 1922, Perloff concluded that "the accusations against the Council on Foreign Relations — the pursuit of world government and receptiveness to communism — are true." He said that the heavy presence of

Council members in Washington has impacted "mightily upon the course of American foreign policy in this century," a disastrous course that "has seen the United States eroded in strength and its allies sometimes vanquished altogether."

Perloff offered convincing evidence that control of the State Department was achieved by the CFR in 1939 and has continued ever since. James Baker was only the second Secretary of State in 45 years who was not a member of the Council when he became Secretary, although his Number Two man, Deputy Secretary Lawrence S. Eagleburger, was. Eagleburger was also a "Former Member in Public Service" of the Trilateral Commission. This continuity in managing U.S. foreign policy was addressed by Barry Goldwater in *With No Apologies* :

> When a new President comes on board, there is a great turnover in personnel but no change in policy. Example: During the Nixon years Henry Kissinger, CFR member and Nelson Rockefeller's protege, was in charge of foreign policy. When Jimmy Carter was elected, Kissinger was replaced by Zbigniew Brzezinski, CFR member and David Rockefeller's protege.

If Goldwater had written his book in 1990 instead of 1979, he could have brought the Kissinger/Brzezinski legacy up to date. While Kissinger held no attention-grabbing position during the Reagan years, he did serve on Reagan's Foreign Intelligence Advisory Board and his policy of "differentiation" — favoring "good" communist governments over "bad" ones with financial, economic, and techological assistance — was carried out under Reagan.

That same policy continued under President Bush thanks to the influence of Lawrence Eagleburger, who left his job as president of Kissinger Associates to become Deputy Secretary of State, and Brent Scowcroft, the CFR and TC member who was vice chairman of Kissinger Associates before joining the Bush Administration as national security advisor to the President. And, as noted earlier, when Mr. Bush was looking for foreign policy advice prior to his election in 1988, he picked as the co-chairmen of his national security task force Gerald Ford, Henry Kissinger, Brent Scowcroft, and Zbigniew Brzezinski. No wonder the nation's policy never changes!

In July 1990, President Bush continued the CFR domination of his Administration by naming four of its members to his six-member intelligence advisory board. Chosen to advise Mr. Bush on intelligence issues were Admiral Bobby R. Inman, Lew Allen Jr., John M. Deutch, and William G. Hyland, who is not only a CFR member but also editor of *Foreign Affairs* .

CFR policies that have proved damaging to the cause of freedom and helpful to the advance of communism have led some critics to accuse CFR members of having links to the international communist conspiracy. In *The Shadows of Power*, James Perloff stated his view that many CFR members are not knowing participants in any worldwide conspiracy. He said that many of them really don't seem to care what the goals of the organization would mean to the independence of the United States and the freedom of the American people.

Barry Goldwater concurs. While the Council's rolls did include at one time such identified communists as Alger Hiss, Lauchlin Currie, and Owen Lattimore, its members, in the opinion of Goldwater, "are indifferent to communism. They have no ideological anchors. In their pursuit of a new world order, they are prepared to deal without prejudice with a communist state, a socialist state, a democratic state, monarchy, oligarchy — it's all the same to them."

The Rockefeller Connection

The career of David Rockefeller, who stepped down as chairman of the CFR in 1986 after 44 years of close association with the Council (he remained as North American chairman of the Trilateral Commission), illustrates Goldwater's point. This international banker has spent most of his adult life propping up and bailing out totalitarian regimes from Angola to Zimbabwe. He sees nothing "immoral or improper with our dealing with people with very diverse views, even if they conduct their affairs in a way that we might even find quite repugnant."

Interviewed by CFR member Bill Moyers during a televised PBS special in 1980, Rockefeller said that "just because a country is technically called communist doesn't mean that a capitalist institution such as the Chase Bank can't deal with them on a mutually beneficial basis, and indeed we do deal with most of the so-called communist countries of the world on a basis that has worked out very well, I think, for both of us."

It works out well for Rockefeller because his bank extends credit to those governments, rakes in the interest while the struggling countries fall deeper into debt, and finances their socialist bureaucracies. U.S. taxpayers even help some of those governments pay the interest on their loans through such institutions as the International Monetary Fund and the World Bank. Thus, the big banks get their money back at the expense of the American taxpayer, conditions are made worse for the suffering people in those debt-ridden countries, and the proponents of one-world government gain more clout.

David Rockefeller has denied being part of what he termed "a small group of people who are somehow gathering together and plotting what should be done for the country." But Bill Moyers, who accompanied the Chase Bank chairman on a one-week visit to the economic and political leaders of five European countries, found it "staggeringly impressive and not a little scary that a relatively small number of global entrepreneurs have accomplished what escaped the League of Nations and the UN — they have, in one way, created one world, governed by the cold logic of profit.... David Rockefeller is the most conspicuous representative today of the ruling class, a multinational fraternity of men who shape the global economy and manage the flow of its capital."

What does Mr. Rockefeller think of George Bush? He told Sidney Blumenthal early in 1988 that "Bush has the knowledge and the background and has had the posts. If he were President, he would be in a better position than anyone else to pull together the people in the country who believe that we are in fact living in one world and have to act that way." A year later, the *Washington Post* said that a Bush Administration meant "the return of the insiders." The Eastern Establishment, said David Ignatius in the *Post*,

> ... is back in power after nearly 20 years in the post-Vietnam wilderness.... The Establishment is back — not just the individuals and the pedigrees, but the state of mind.... In Bush's Washington, government is no longer regarded as the enemy. It is seen again, as it was 25 years ago, as a venue for doing good in the world, for promoting virtue. It seeks a kinder, gentler — and less political — America.

When Vice President Bush was asked by *Conservative Digest* in 1986 about the CFR and TC, he replied: "I really haven't kept up with them. President Reagan had the Trilateral Commission to the White House. I missed that meeting. But the idea that they are subversive organizations is absolutely crazy." Asked if they were "liberal, moderate, conservative, non-ideological," Bush said: "I think it's hard to say when you have a membership that goes from one end of the political spectrum to the other. In both of these organizations I would agree with some people who are members and violently disagree with others."

But when Sidney Blumenthal asked Rockefeller in 1988 about Bush's resignation from the TC and the CFR, David responded: "I don't know what I would have done. I don't think he really accomplished what he hoped. It was still used against him. He has since spoken to the Council and the Trilateral and has been fully supportive of their activities. Even though he has resigned, he hasn't walked away from them."

Indeed he hasn't, since the CFR lists 350 of its members as officials of the Bush Administration. Presumably they are people with whom the President does not violently disagree, such as Secretary of Defense Dick Cheney, Secretary of the Treasury Nicholas Brady, Attorney General Richard Thornburgh, and CIA Director William Webster. And the TC lists as "Former Members in Public Service," in addition to Bush, Scowcroft, and Eagleburger, Office of Management and Budget Director Richard Darman (CFR), Federal Reserve Chairman Alan Greenspan (CFR), and Special Trade Representative Carla Hills.

That is quite a significant representation in government for the CFR, whose entire membership is approximately 2,500, and for the TC, which has fewer than 100 members in the United States. Candidate Bush made a big issue in the 1988 campaign about Democrat Michael Dukakis' membership in the American Civil Liberties Union. It's too bad that just as big a deal was not made of the Republican nominee's connections with two organizations of equal danger to America's national security. That the indictment of George Bush was not made may well be attributed to the overwhelming presence of CFR members in top media posts.

And by the way, if anyone thinks that the CFR might not have had as much influence in a Dukakis Administration, be advised that Governor Dukakis later joined the organization himself and was first listed as a member in the CFR's Annual Report dated June 30, 1989.

His rhetoric to the contrary notwithstanding, George Bush has been directly or indirectly involved with internationalists at least since his senior year at Yale. It was then that he belonged to Skull and Bones, the secret Yale fraternity that writer and lecturer Gary Allen once described as "the nexus of an 'old boy' network which is at the heart of what is known as the Eastern Liberal Establishment." Allen said that Skull and Bones "appears to act as a recruiting ground for the international banking clique, the CIA, and politics."

Other Bonesmen who have achieved national prominence include William Howard Taft, Henry Luce, Potter Stewart, McGeorge Bundy, William F. Buckley Jr., Winston Lord, and Senators David Boren, John Chafee, and John Kerry.

The United Nations

Both before and after his brief tenure at the United Nations in the early Seventies, Mr. Bush has been a supporter of the UN. While that body never has lived up "to its original expectations," he said in his autobiography, "the UN still serves a valuable purpose. It may be largely ineffective — and sometimes counterproductive — in the political area. But UN peacekeeping forces have performed well, from Korea in the early 1950s to the Middle East in the 1970s and '80s. And the organization's efforts in science, medicine, agriculture, and space technology — not to mention its humanitarian work providing for refugees and feeding the hungry — have been indispensable."

There is plenty of historical evidence to contradict even that qualified endorsement, as many observers have pointed out. For instance, Robert W. Lee, in his scholarly book *The United Nations Conspiracy*, made clear that the UN is a "judas goat" that is "taking us down the garden path toward a Marxist-oriented world government."

Among other things, Lee noted that Alger Hiss, later exposed as a Soviet spy, was the secretary general of the UN's founding conference in San Francisco in 1945; that Secretary General U Thant in 1970 praised Lenin as a leader whose "ideals of peace and peaceful coexistence among states have won widespread international acceptance and they are in line with the aims of the UN Charter"; and that Secretary General Kurt Waldheim was a Nazi foot soldier during World War II.

Lee also discussed the UN's role in preventing victory over the communists in the Korean War; the murderous assaults by UN "peacekeeping" forces on hospitals, churches, and innocent civilians in the Congolese province of Katanga in 1961; aid to communist forces in Vietnam from the United Nations Children's Fund (UNICEF); and numerous other examples of UN assistance for communists while it fiercely opposed anti-communists.

But in November 1989, the United States and the Soviet Union agreed to sponsor a resolution in the General Assembly calling for the UN to play a greater role in maintaining peace and fostering international cooperation. A joint statement issued by the two governments said that "what is most important about this resolution is not its specific language but what it symbolizes as a new beginning at the United Nations — a new spirit of constructive cooperation."

That cooperation manifested itself after Iraq's seizure of Kuwait in August 1990 when the United States joined with the USSR and a score of other nations in backing the UN Security Council's economic sanctions against Iraq. "We are now in sight of a United Nations that performs as envisioned by its founders," said President Bush on September 11, 1990. That is not good news for America when one considers that the founders of the UN envisioned submerging a sovereign United States in a supranational government.

World Government

While he may have severed his formal ties with the Council on Foreign Relations and the Trilateral Commission, President Bush and those around him continue to work for what he described on September 11th as his "dream of a new world order," which is just a euphemism for world government. In theory, a world government based on truth, justice, freedom, and peace would be wonderful. But looking around the globe today, how many world leaders do we see who really understand and believe in truth, justice, freedom, and peace? To put the United States at the mercy of those who do not share our aspirations and ideals would be suicidal.

There are four certain consequences of a world government ruled by a powerful clique, said John F. McManus in his 1983 book *The Insiders*:

> One: Rather than improve the standard of living for other nations, world government will mean a forced redistribution of all wealth and a sharp reduction in the standard of living for Americans.
>
> Two: Strict regimentation will become commonplace, and there will no longer be any freedom of movement, freedom of worship, private property rights, free speech, or the right to publish.
>
> Three: World government will mean that this once glorious land of opportunity will become another socialistic nightmare where no amount of effort will produce just reward.
>
> Four: World order will be enforced by agents of the world government in the same way that agents of the Kremlin enforce their rule throughout Soviet Russia today.

Back in 1953, Norman Dodd was director of research for a congressional committee headed by Representative Carroll Reece of Tennessee. The committee had been formed for the purpose of investigating the promotion of world government and socialism by the powerful tax-exempt foundations. Dodd was invited to the headquarters of the Ford Foundation by its president, H. Rowan Gaither, who was a member of the CFR. "Mr. Dodd," Gaither told him, "all of us here at the policymaking level have had experience, either in O.S.S. [Office of Strategic Services] or the European Economic Administration, with directives from the White House. We operate under those directives here. Would you like to know what those directives are?"

When Dodd said that he would, Gaither continued: "The substance of them is that we shall use our grant-making power so to alter life in the United States that we can be comfortably merged with the Soviet Union." A startled Dodd asked if Gaither would be willing to repeat that before the Reece Committee, but the Ford Foundation president replied: "That we would not think of doing."

Premeditated Merger

There is considerable evidence that such a merger remains a very real possibility. Life in the United States has indeed been altered in recent decades in the direction of an all-powerful central government that would merge very smoothly with the Soviet Union, or with a united Europe. Speaking at Texas A & M University on May 12, 1989, President Bush said, "We seek the integration of the Soviet Union into the community of nations.... Ultimately, our objective is to welcome the Soviet Union back into the world order." His remarks came just five months after Mikhail Gorbachev had told the UN General Assembly that "further world progress is only possible through a search for universal human consensus as we move forward to a new world order."

In a December 12, 1989 speech at the West Berlin Press Club, Secretary of State James Baker called for "a new architecture" that would encompass both Western and communist Europe. He said that this new architecture "must continue the construction of institutions — like the European

Community — that can help draw together the West while also serving as an open door to the East. And the new architecture must build up frameworks ... that can overcome the division of Europe and bridge the Atlantic Ocean."

The following month, William Taft, the permanent U.S. representative to NATO, told a conference in Paris that the Bush Administration favored the establishment of a worldwide defense market that would "combine the industrial bases of North America, East Asia, and Europe into a single Western industrial base." Taft said that such a market would allow the defense ministries of those countries to "integrate their purchases of weapons systems."

On March 7, 1990, Zbigniew Brzezinski authored an Op-Ed piece in the *New York Times* urging a European policy "founded upon the grand concept of a trans-European commonwealth with the European Community at its core but embracing Central Europe and being open also to eventual association with the Soviet Union." Brzezinski had spoken at the Soviet Foreign Ministry Diplomatic Academy in Moscow the previous October and had called for cooperation between NATO and the Warsaw Pact to bring about "a larger European security system" that "could help to preserve geopolitical and territorial stability while permitting political and economic change. We must create institutionalized economic lines, including cross-cutting membership in security and other cooperative organizations."

This is the same Zbigniew Brzezinski who declared in his 1970 book, *Between Two Ages*, that "national sovereignty is no longer a viable concept," and who suggested piecemeal "movement toward a larger community of the developed nations ... through a variety of indirect ties and already developing limitations on national sovereignty." In the October 1970 issue of *Foreign Affairs*, Brzezinski said that this community of the developed nations should include the United States, Western Europe, and Japan. He returned to the subject in the July 1973 issue of *Foreign Affairs*, saying that "without closer American-European-Japanese cooperation the major problems of today cannot be effectively tackled, and ... *the active promotion of such trilateral cooperation must now become the central priority of U.S. policy.*" (Emphasis in the original.)

David Rockefeller then chose Brzezinski to be director of the Trilateral Commission, the two of them groomed Jimmy Carter as their ideal presidential candidate, the Trilaterals got one of their own in the White House in 1976, and the active promotion of Trilateralism has continued ever since.

"A new world order is taking shape so fast that governments as well as private citizens find it difficult just to absorb 'the gallop of events,' " wrote Don Oberdorfer in the February 25, 1990 *Washington Post*. Citing the pending unification of Germany, the upheaval in communist Europe, and the crisis in the Soviet Union, Oberdorfer said that since the Malta summit in December 1989, "the policy of the Bush Administration has been openly to support Gorbachev's perestroika policies and, increasingly, Gorbachev himself. The cooperative relationship between Washington and Moscow, strikingly different from that of previous decades, now includes conscious U.S. efforts not to confront or embarrass the Soviet leaders as they continue their reformist ways."

Those conscious efforts were very much in evidence when Gorbachev came to Washington on May 31, 1990, for a four-day visit to the United States. After signing or agreeing to sign 15 accords, protocols, and statements that would benefit the Soviet Union at the expense of the United States, President Bush hailed those "reforms that make our systems more compatible on the economic side, on the human rights side, the openness side. But we're not looking for, trying to achieve advantage." Small wonder that Gorbachev responded by saying that Mr. Bush was "the kind of person to do business with, to build our relations with."

George Bush seems willing to skip over seven decades of Soviet barbarism that murdered scores of millions outside of military conflicts. In his determined effort to "welcome the Soviet Union back into the world order," he has ignored the Gorbachev-led rape of Afghanistan, thousands of still-operating slave labor camps and psychiatric prisons, continuing worldwide KGB operations, military and economic sustenance for revolutionaries in Africa and Central America, and the strangled cries for freedom and independence from Lithuania and other captured lands.

Refusal even to ostracize the unrepentant purveyors of monstrous crimes invites additional criminal activity. Why should the crimes of Nazi Germany continue to earn condemnation if President Bush has no apparent compunction about sweeping the more numerous and unceasing crimes of Soviet rulers under a red carpet?

Edith Kermit Roosevelt called the Establishment the "legitimate Mafia."

Foreign Affairs spells out the elitist program of the internationalists.

The Harold Pratt House at 58 East 68th Street in New York City is the headquarters of the CFR and the site of many of its private meetings.

David Rockefeller said
George Bush and he share
common beliefs.

Zbigniew Brzezinski was
the first U.S. director of
the Trilateral Commission.

President Jimmy Carter meeting with his cabinet officers,
many of whom were Trilateralists and CFR members.

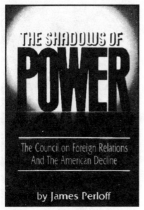

James Perloff's book offers proof of CFR's pursuit of world rule.

Barry Goldwater warned about CFR domination of U.S. foreign policy.

Bill Moyers said David Rockefeller and friends are a ruling class.

Henry Kissinger heavily influences America's foreign policy plans.

The chairman of the Federal Reserve is CFR member Alan Greenspan.

CFR member Richard Cheney holds the top post in the Pentagon.

CFR member Nicholas Brady is Mr. Bush's Treasury Secretary.

Attorney General Dick Thornburgh is another member of the CFR.

A.P./Wide World Photos

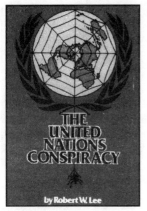

Robert Lee wrote about
the UN's role in
leading U.S. into
world government.

Alger Hiss was secretary
general of UN's founding
meeting in San Francisco.

UN Secretary General U
Thant once praised Lenin
as an idealist for peace.

Rowan Gaither told of
directives to bring about
merger with Soviet Union.

Chapter 5
The Interventionist

We would be inclined probably to follow the example of France who today has said that if the Warsaw Pact felt it necessary to intervene in behalf of the opposition [in Romania], they would support that action.

— Secretary of State James Baker,
December 24, 1989

Even some liberals must have been startled when Secretary Baker invited the Soviet Union and its military allies to intervene in Romania following the overthrow of Nicolae Ceausescu, the communist tyrant who had brutalized the Romanian people for 24 years. While being interviewed on the December 24, 1989 airing of NBC's *Meet the Press*, Baker said that "we would support efforts to assist the Popular Front for National Salvation there in Romania. They are attempting to put off the yoke of a very, very oppressive and repressive dictatorship." He then said that the Bush Administration "would be inclined probably to follow the example of France who today has said that if the Warsaw Pact felt it necessary to intervene in behalf of the opposition, they would support that action."

It was bad enough that it took Mr. Baker this long to concede the evil nature of a Ceausescu regime that his boss, George Bush, had praised so highly just six years earlier; it was even worse that he was giving the Warsaw Pact, the Soviet military alliance, the green light to keep Romania under communist rule. "Apparently," said David Funderburk, U.S. Ambassador to Romania from 1981 to 1985, "Baker did not know that the USSR occupies the Romanian provinces of Bessarabia and northern Bucovina, and had originally superimposed the alien communism on the Romanians with tanks and troops and non-Romanian Communist Party agents. Romanians resent the Soviets, whom they consider slavemasters and occupiers, and were thus appalled that Washington could recommend the use of Soviet and Warsaw Pact troops to Romania."

Recalling Mr. Bush's visit to Bucharest in September 1983, Dr. Funderburk said that the Vice President held Ceausescu up "as a model in Eastern Europe to be favored, when Bush knew of the repressive, murderous reality of Ceausescu's regime." Bush knew because Funderburk had frequently and officially urged, in dispatches and during personal communication with a variety of Reagan Administration officials, that the United States cease any aid to or praise for Ceausescu and his barbaric comrades.

Stopping in Vienna during that same 1983 trip to communist Europe, Bush enunciated Henry Kissinger's policy of "differentiation" (but not liberation) in a speech drafted for him by the State Department's Lawrence Eagleburger and Mark Palmer:

> The United States will engage in closer political, economic, and cultural relations with those countries, such as Hungary and Romania, which assert greater openness or independence. We will not, however, reward closed societies and belligerent foreign policies — countries such as Bulgaria and Czechoslovakia, which continue to violate the most fundamental human rights; and countries such as East Germany and, again, Bulgaria, which act as proxies to the Soviets in the training, funding, and arming of terrorists.

After Nicolae Ceausescu and his wife were executed on Christmas Day in 1989, the world learned many gory details about the incredible cruelty and bizarre behavior they had inflicted on the Romanian people. But this information had been known for years to U.S. government officials, who nevertheless fawned over Ceausescu and ignored his Stalinist actions. Let Ambassador Funderburk describe what George Bush and the State Department chose to ignore. Additional details can be found in his 1987 book *Pinstripes and Reds*:

During my tenure as U.S. Ambassador to Romania, our embassy reported many of the horrors that typified Ceausescu's rule: demolition of churches, murder of priests and pastors and political dissidents, and the jailing of opponents throughout the country. A vast gulag of slave labor worked on the Danube-Black Sea Canal. Hit squads were sent out to eliminate enemies, including broadcasters for Radio Free Europe in Munich. The U.S. Embassy was radiated, and American Embassy employees' houses were bugged and their telephones tapped.

Ceausescu sold thousands of Jews to Israel and Germans to West Germany for $10,000 to $15,000 per person (much of which went into Swiss bank accounts). The Romanian Communists provided training facilities and safe haven for radical Arab terrorists; at one time in the1980s Romania was the fifth largest military armaments exporter in the world (mainly to other communists and to radical Arab states).

Ceausescu himself required total fealty from his subjects, even to the extent that he demanded to be referred to as god. Given his destructive policies and state-ordered murders, he must be ranked with Pol Pot, Stalin, Mao, and Hitler.

Yet Ceausescu received from the United States Most Favored Nation trade status from 1975 to 1988, when he himself, not the Reagan Administration, demanded that it be terminated. But the chances of a change for the better for the Romanian people were lessened in May 1990 when Ion Iliescu stole the election for president of the country. Iliescu, who had studied with Mikhail Gorbachev in Moscow, was Communist Party secretary under Ceausescu in the 1970s, and his National Salvation Front, which James Baker wanted to save with Soviet troops and tanks, was dominated by the same communists who had ruled the country under Ceausescu.

The situation in the other communist nations of Central and Eastern Europe, despite media reports to the contrary, was not much better. More than half a million Soviet troops remained in those nations in the fall of 1990 and Gorbachev showed no signs of keeping his promise to withdraw them soon. Furthermore, communists or "reformers" sympathetic to communism, or its evil twin socialism, were still calling the shots, and the Bush-Baker team was intervening on their side rather than the side of the victimized people. Consider some examples.

Czechoslovakia

The new leader of Czechoslovakia was playwright-turned-politician Vaclav Havel, who was welcomed to Washington in February 1990 by President Bush and promised Most Favored Nation trade status, Export-Import Bank low-cost loans, and support for Czech admission to the International Monetary Fund and World Bank. Havel, who admitted that old-line communists still controlled most of the government ministries and made it difficult to push through any legitimate reforms, also made a curious statement in his address to a joint session of Congress:

I often hear the question, How can the United States

of America help us today? My reply is as paradoxical as the whole of my life has been. You can help us most of all if you help the Soviet Union on its irreversible but immensely complicated road to democracy.

There were other paradoxes as well. For instance, just before he became president of Czechoslovakia in December 1989, Havel proclaimed over Czech television: "For 20 years it was official propaganda that I was the enemy of socialism, that I wanted to bring back capitalism, that I was in the service of imperialism. All those were lies." Though never a communist himself, he accepted the backing of communist Alexander Dubcek, a former Czech ruler, saying that "by my side, in whatever function, will stand Alexander Dubcek," and of former Communist Party Secretary Cestmir Cisar, who said, "I know the qualifications of Mr. Havel.... I tell you his programs and mine are in many points one and the same."

Living under socialism for 40 years in Czechoslovakia can cloud one's vision. Instead of throwing off the yoke of socialism entirely, and giving the suffering people the freedom to make their own way in the world, the so-called reformers seemed to favor a more benign socialism, the democratic variety practiced in Western Europe rather than the totalitarian version imposed on the Soviet Union. But concentration of all political and economic power in the hands of the state will not remain benign for very long. Those in power like telling people what to do ("Power tends to corrupt and absolute power corrupts absolutely" — Lord Acton) and, sooner or later, they will resort to force to maintain their primacy and privileges.

That is why any enthusiasm over the alleged "collapse of communism" must be tempered with reality. Technically speaking, true communism, which its theorists define as the withering away of the state, does not exist anywhere in the world today. No one should ever forget that USSR means

Union of Soviet *Socialist* Republics. What has killed more than 100 million people in this century is totalitarian socialism. So if Gorbachev were to announce the abolition of communism tomorrow, his pronouncement would not mean the end of socialism's threat to freedom; it would mean only that the threat had been given a different name.

East Germany

Someone wisely observed that the Berlin Wall was built in 1961 to keep the people in and it was torn down in 1989 for the same reason. The exodus of East German citizens through Hungary and Czechoslovakia would have been even greater had the wall remained. But once East Germans began to believe they could cross back and forth freely into West Berlin and West Germany, many decided to stay. The exodus also served a couple of communist purposes: it got rid of dissidents and troublemakers who were constantly agitating against the regime, and it allowed the infiltration of communist agents into other countries.

But despite the media hoopla over the tearing down of the wall, things changed slowly in East Germany. Nearly 400,000 Soviet troops remained there, and the new rulers at first bore a strong resemblance to their hardline predecessors. It was naive to think that communists would walk easily away from power accumulated over the years. The catalyst in organizing opposition to the old regime was a group called New Forum, which was created in September 1989. The group's thinking could be gauged by listening to Jens Reich, one of its co-founders: "I think that the majority of our followers are against a capitalist society. They would prefer to have our socialist building reconstructed, reformed in a way that is acceptable to the majority of the population."

None of this would come as a surprise to Anatoliy Golitsyn, a former KGB official who defected to the Free World in 1961 and wrote a book (*New Lies for Old*) in 1984 predicting that communist strategists seeking "the complete triumph of communism" would introduce a "false liberalization in Eastern Europe and, probably, in the Soviet Union and the exhibition of spurious independence on the part of the regimes in Romania, Czechoslovakia, and Poland."

Getting even more specific five years before the events actually transpired, Golitsyn said that this "liberalization" in Eastern Europe "would probably involve the return to power in Czechoslovakia of Dubcek and his associates. If it should be extended to East Germany, demolition of the Berlin Wall might even be contemplated." He said that "pressure could well grow for a solution of the German problem in which some form of confederation between East and West Germany would be combined with neutralization of the whole and a treaty of friendship with the Soviet Union. France and Italy, under united front governments, would throw in their lot with Germany and the Soviet Union. Britain would be confronted with a choice between a neutral Europe and the United States."

The confederation between East and West Germany became a reality on July 1, 1990, when the divided nations merged their economic, social, and monetary systems. And the neutralization process picked up speed on July 6th when representatives of the 16 NATO nations, meeting in London, issued a communique stating that "we will never in any circumstances be the first to use force" in case of war and will use nuclear weapons only as a "last resort"; inviting the Warsaw Pact countries to "establish regular diplomatic liaison with NATO"; and proposing that NATO shift from a military to a political alliance and function as "an agent of change" in helping "build the structures of a more united continent."

President Bush viewed the NATO summit meeting as "a historic turning point" for the alliance and as a "vindication" of Gorbachev's policies. He surmised that the Soviet ruler might well be saying to himself: "We've been right to reach out ... to the United States ... to improve relations with Western Europe. They are now changing their doctrine as a result of changes that I, Mr. Gorbachev, have made."

Ten days later, on July 16th, Gorbachev and West German Chancellor Helmut Kohl agreed to let a united Germany join NATO. Kohl had already agreed to pay the expenses of the approximately 380,000 Soviet troops stationed in East Germany until their withdrawal, which Gorbachev said might not be for at least three to four years. Those expenses were estimated at $780 million just for the last six months of 1990.

The "new architecture" in Europe that Secretary of State James Baker had called for during a December 1989 speech in West Berlin was well underway by the middle of 1990. What worried some conservatives, however, was the strong possibility that this new architecture would be a stepping-stone to world government. In his 1942 book *Marxism and the National Question*, Soviet dictator Josef Stalin urged:

> Divide the world into regional groups as a transitional stage to world government. Populations will more readily abandon their national loyalties to a vague regional loyalty than they will for a world authority. Later, the regionals can be brought all the way into a single world dictatorship.

In 1980, NATO Secretary General Joseph Luns echoed Stalin when he said that "the slowly but steadily advancing unity of Europe is the most promising guarantee of our ideals of world government." But opponents of world government, such as John F. McManus, have a better idea. "Instead of plunging more deeply into the entangling clutches of NATO and other 'regional groups,' the U.S. should withdraw and begin again to act as a sovereign entity," McManus wrote in the July 30, 1990 issue of *The New American*. "Let Europeans pay their own defense bills. Let them, if they must, speed toward socialist destruction alone. But let us return to what made us great — a system of limited government and free enterprise in a truly independent United States of America."

Poland

Anatoliy Golitsyn's amazingly accurate 1984 predictions involved Poland as well. He said that the first two phases of communist strategy — creation of Solidarity, followed by imposition of martial law by the Jaruzelski regime and suspension of Solidarity — were "intended to bring the movement under firm control and to provide a period of political consolidation." In the third phase, Golitsyn continued, "it may be expected that a coalition government will be formed, comprising representatives of the communist party, of a revived Solidarity movement, and of the church. A few so-called liberals might also be included."

Talking about events that were still in the future, Golitsyn said that "a coalition government in Poland would in fact be totalitarianism under a new, deceptive, and more dangerous guise. Accepted as the spontaneous emergence of a new form of multiparty, semidemocratic regime, it would serve to undermine resistance to communism inside and outside the communist bloc. The need for massive defense expenditure would increasingly be questioned in the West.... If 'liberalization' is successful and accepted by the West as genuine, it may well be followed by the apparent withdrawal of one or more communist countries from the Warsaw Pact to serve as a model of a 'neutral' socialist state for the whole of Europe to follow."

Golitsyn was able to make these predictions because he knew of the strong communist presence in Solidarity. He said that one of the top communists in Poland, Stanislaw Kania, had revealed that there were one million Communist Party members in Solidarity, that 42 of the party's 200-member

Central Committee in 1981 were Solidarity members, that Bogdan Lis, Lech Walesa's deputy, was a Central Committee member, and that Zofia Gryzb, another Solidarity leader, was a member of the Politburo.

According to the former KGB officer, "these leaders were not expelled from the party for their membership in Solidarity. On the contrary, Solidarity recognized the leading role of the party and the party recognized Solidarity's existence." He said that Solidarity enjoyed access to the state-controlled media and "obstacles were not placed in the way of Walesa's extensive foreign travels; indeed, the Polish ambassador to Japan, who defected after the introduction of martial law, assisted in arranging Walesa's contacts with Japanese trade unions."

George Bush has been in close touch with the situation in Poland at least since 1981, when he was named head of a "Special Situation Group" to monitor events in that country following the imposition of martial law. He visited Poland in September 1987 and agreed with Jaruzelski to help his regime seek rescheduling of its $35 billion foreign debt with the Club of Paris creditors. Mr. Bush also met with Walesa and expressed his support for Solidarity.

In April 1989, President Bush announced an eight-point aid package for Poland and said that "Poland offers two lessons for all. First, there can be no progress without significant political and economic liberalization. And second, help from the West will come in concert with liberalization." He visited the country again in July 1989, promising hundreds of millions of dollars in aid and loans and saluting Jaruzelski "for his leadership and his extraordinary hospitality to me." And he welcomed Polish Prime Minister Tadeusz Mazowiecki to the White House in March 1990 for the signing of a trade agreement giving Western businesses the same legal rights in Poland as in non-communist countries. The pact was "a milestone on the road to a prosperous Poland," said Mr. Bush.

The United States had sent more than $3 billion in aid and credits, and better than $2 billion in food assistance, to Poland in the two decades preceding the alleged changes there in 1989, but the nation's problems were just as bad as ever. This should have been expected since the aid went to the bankrupt communist regime that had caused the problems in the first place, and that regime used the assistance to continue rather than correct its corrupt programs. Stanton Evans tells why change is so difficult in a socialist system:

> These societies, to take an obvious case in point, have millions of bureaucrats and workers in subsidized, state-run enterprises who are employed on uneconomic projects, and who would be inexorably displaced in a market-driven, competitive system. They also typically have huge, repressed inflations from all the official overspending, resulting in price controls that make goods seem cheap but lock the gears of the economy, causing misallocation of resources and chronic shortages.
>
> All of this needs to be changed if the states in question are to develop productive economic systems — along with conversion to private banking and investment institutions, privatization of state-run enterprises, and so on.

Congress gave final approval in November 1989 to an $852 million aid package to Poland that included $125 million in food assistance, $240 million in grants to private businesses, $200 million to bolster the Polish monetary unit (the zloty), and $200 million in U.S. taxpayer-guaranteed loans to Polish companies desiring to import American products. During debate on the package, Congress agreed to an amendment introduced by Senator William Armstrong (R-CO) conditioning the aid on Poland's halting the shipment of arms to communist and other repressive regimes around the world.

According to Armstrong, the Polish regime had "shipped an enormous amount of war materiel" to Cuba, at least $130 million worth from 1982 to 1987, as well as $50 million in arms to Angola, $50 million to Libya, $2.5 million to the Soviet Union, and undisclosed amounts to Nicaragua, North Korea, Vietnam, Iraq, and Iran. "Poland is the seventh-ranking country in the world in supplying military arms to regimes, some of which are simply despicable," said Senator Armstrong. But his amendment was dropped from the bill during a House-Senate conference.

In his State of the Union address on January 31, 1990, President Bush remarked: "A year ago in Poland, Lech Walesa declared that he was ready to open a dialogue with the communist rulers of that country. Today, with the future of a free Poland in their own hands, members of Solidarity lead the Polish government." As noted earlier, that simply was not true. Non-communist Mazowiecki may have been the Prime Minister, but communists controlled the military, the police, the secret police, the courts, and local governments. "President" Wojciech Jaruzelski, the hardline communist who had imposed martial law in 1981, retained the authority to dismiss the Prime Minister, dissolve Parliament, declare martial law, and ratify international agreements. Poland remained dominated by communists.

Though he was the object of high praise during a triumphal visit to the United States in November 1989 that included an address to a joint session of Congress, Lech Walesa was not revered by all. One critic, for example, was Anna Walentynowicz, a veteran of 32 years of work in the Gdansk shipyard and a woman known as the mother of Solidarity. She told American audiences that after Walesa assumed leadership of Solidarity in 1980, he still maintained close contacts with top communists and received special favors from them.

She said that the communists helped make him an internationally famous figure and that he ousted all true Polish patriots from positions of influence within the Solidarity trade union.

So unhappy were anti-communist Poles with the deal Walesa worked out with the communists for the June 1989 elections — the people of Poland would be allowed to choose 35 percent of the seats in the lower chamber of Parliament and 100 percent of the seats in the upper chamber while Jaruzelski would become a president with dictatorial powers — that 38 percent of them boycotted the elections, said Walentynowicz. That meant, she said, that "38 percent of the electorate voted decisively against Walesa's policies." And these were people who for a long time had wanted desperately to vote in a truly free election.

Yet, Walesa continued to solicit aid from the Free World, she said, even though "under present circumstances, additional credits [will] strengthen the regime without solving any of the problems that plague the Polish economy.... Poland needs freedom and not Western credits." The truth is, said Walentynowicz, that "Lech Walesa no longer represents the interests of the people of Poland. By accepting accommodation with the regime, he voluntarily deprived himself of the right to speak on behalf of the nation."

Like Vaclav Havel, Lech Walesa has made statements that disturb those who want genuine freedom from communism. Early in 1989, for instance, Walesa said in an interview with the Soviet magazine *New Times*: "Let power remain in the hands of the communists, but let it be different. Let it serve the people better, respect the law, and be accountable to society. We are prepared to cooperate constructively with such authorities." And talking to reporters from another Soviet publication, *Ogonyok*, in August of 1989, Walesa said, "We want to take a lot from capitalism — what is good for the people, what the people will take from it. But we also want to take what's good from socialism."

Nicaragua

On May 25, 1990, President Bush signed into law a bill that would send $420 million in aid to Panama and $300 million to Nicaragua, both of which had new governments due to direct intervention by the U.S. government in the case of Panama, and indirect intervention in the case of Nicaragua. The Carter Administration had forced Nicaragua's anti-communist ruler, Anastasio Somoza, out of power in 1979 and helped impose a brutal Sandinista communist regime on the Nicaraguan people.

Elections in February 1990 turned the Sandinistas out of office, but before the new government of former Sandinista Violeta Barrios de Chamorro took power in April, the Sandinistas solidified themselves in the government bureaucracy, the civil service unions, and the universities. They began almost immediately after the Chamorro inauguration to stage paralyzing strikes and make the country ungovernable, carrying out the promise of ousted communist President Daniel Ortega to "rule from below" despite his electoral defeat.

Mrs. Chamorro made her situation even more tenuous by keeping Humberto Ortega, Daniel's hardline communist brother, as head of the powerful Nicaraguan army. She also allowed El Salvador's communist terrorist force, the FMLN, to keep its office in Managua, having been influenced in that decision by two of her children and a nephew, all of whom had close ties with the FMLN. The early months of her tenure also saw the murder by Sandinistas of former Contras and their families who had surrendered their arms after getting promises of safety, food, housing, and jobs. The Contras were the anti-communist fighters who had tried unsuccessfully for a decade to restore freedom to Nicaragua by overthrowing the Sandinistas.

During the decade of Sandinista rule, the Reagan-Bush Administration talked a lot about helping the Contras get rid of the Sandinistas, but never fought hard enough with Congress for the quantity of military arms and equipment that might have enabled the freedom fighters to achieve victory. They gave the Contras just enough assistance to get many of them killed, but not enough to defeat the communist forces who were receiving massive arms support from the Soviet Union. The Administration's goal, said President Reagan on August 5, 1986, was not "a purely military solution," but rather to give the Contras "leverage to bring the communists to the table and negotiate a political, and democratic, peace."

Interviewed by a Miami radio station in August 1987, Vice President Bush said, "We are not going to leave the Contras twisting in the wind, wondering whether they are going to be done in by a peace plan." Yet that is exactly what happened. Two years later, as President, Mr. Bush made repeated appeals to the Soviet Union to stop sending arms to Cuba and Nicaragua, some of which were being passed along to the FMLN forces in El Salvador, including Soviet-made SAM-7 missiles, rocket-propelled grenades and launchers, automatic rifles, and ammunition.

In a Thanksgiving Eve speech to the nation in 1989, Mr. Bush charged that Cuba and Nicaragua were "holding out against their people only because of the massive support of weapons and supplies from their communist allies." He said that when he saw Gorbachev at Malta two weeks from then, "I'll ask him to join with us to help bring freedom and democracy to all the people of Latin America."

But when asked about arms to El Salvador at a joint news conference with Gorbachev in Malta on December 3rd, the President replied:

> I don't believe that the Sandinistas have told the truth to our Soviet friends. And why? Because we know for a fact that certain arms have gone in there. I'm not saying they're Soviet arms. They've said they aren't

shipping arms and I'm accepting that. But they're going in there, and I am saying that they have misled Mr. Shevardnadze [the Soviet Foreign Minister] when they gave a specific representation that no arms were going from Nicaragua into El Salvador.

Gorbachev must have had a tough time keeping a straight face while Mr. Bush talked about the Sandinistas lying to "our Soviet friends" and about his acceptance of Gorbachev's word that the USSR was not shipping arms to the region when there was an abundance of evidence to the contrary. The pipeline from the Soviet Union, through Cuba and Nicaragua, to El Salvador had been in existence for years. A plane originating in Managua and carrying 24 Soviet SAM-7 missiles had crashed in El Salvador just eight days before the Malta news conference. Letting Gorbachev off that particular hook was typical of George Bush's continued efforts to create a nice-guy image for the ruthless and dangerous Kremlin ruler.

Panama

The Bush Administration's next intervention in Latin America occurred on December 20, 1989, when the President sent 12,000 U.S. military personnel (in addition to the 13,000 already stationed at U.S. bases in the country) into Panama to overthrow the dictatorial regime of Manuel Noriega. The invasion was necessary, Mr. Bush said, "to safeguard the lives of Americans, to defend democracy in Panama, to combat drug trafficking, and to protect the integrity of the Panama Canal treaty." He said that "General Noriega's reckless threats and attacks upon Americans in Panama created an imminent danger to the 35,000 American citizens in Panama. As President, I have no higher obligation than to safeguard the lives of American citizens."

Twenty-three Americans were killed in the invasion and

323 were wounded, and all the invading troops were withdrawn from Panama by the following February. Noriega escaped capture at first and sought asylum at the Vatican Embassy before finally surrendering to U.S. authorities on January 3rd. He was indicted in Miami on a variety of charges, including receiving more than $4.6 million to protect cocaine shipments from Colombia through Panama to the United States.

Just after the invasion, President Bush said that "the revitalization of the Panamanian economy is a major priority in the months ahead, as are our efforts for humanitarian assistance." He asked for $1 billion in economic help for Panama in January 1990, and another $500 million to be taken from the U.S. defense budget in March, before signing an aid bill worth $420 million in May. The aid can be expected to do what most of the hundreds of billions of U.S. foreign aid dollars have done since the end of World War II, that is, finance socialist governments, build bureaucracies, and install and maintain petty dictators in power, earning for the United States not praise and gratitude from the people in the recipient nations, but rather hatred and contempt. This aid request also raised the question of how a country with a $3 trillion national debt could afford to continue sending billions of dollars to other nations.

Then there was the question of sending U.S. troops into foreign countries for reasons other than to protect the lives of American citizens. Where did Mr. Bush get the authority to commit American military personnel to such causes as defending "democracy" and combatting drug trafficking? What's to prevent him from sending Americans to bring about democracy in other countries? If that is his mission, why not try to restore democracy to Cuba or Iran or even Red China? Why the selective intervention in Panama?

Actually, if getting rid of Noriega were the right course — and the evidence to justify such U.S. intervention is sorely lacking — sending in American troops could have been avoided if the President had followed through in October 1989 with his promise to help officers of the Panamanian Defense Force (PDF) capture the Panamanian dictator. Bush had encouraged the PDF to overthrow Noriega in May of that year and, when the time for the coup came, the PDF officers asked to have U.S. soldiers block three roads so forces loyal to Noriega could not maneuver to protect him.

The PDF rebels captured the dictator on October 3rd and held him for several hours, waiting for U.S. authorities to come and get him. But no one came and, because U.S. forces failed to block one of the roads, Noriega's men rescued him and killed the leaders of the coup. The PDF opposition had even called the office of Senator Jesse Helms (R-NC) in Washington to confirm that they had Noriega. But when Helms called the White House to alert the President to the situation, he was told that all top Administration officials were tied up at meetings with foreign visitors, such as Soviet Defense Minister Dmitri Yazov and Mexican President Carlos Salinas de Gortari.

The day after Senator Helms told the Senate about his call from Panama, Mr. Bush said that "there was never a chance" to have Noriega handed over to the United States. "There was a report that he was offered to our military and they wouldn't take him," the President said. "Well, that simply isn't true. Obviously, I would like to see him out, but I think any Commander-in-Chief must have the lives of American citizens and of American soldiers foremost in mind when he makes a decision." His decision to invade Panama two and a half months later cost 23 American lives.

South Africa

There is no country that demonstrates better the bankruptcy of the Bush Administration's interventionist policies than South Africa. Let it be said that South Africa's policy of government-enforced racial separation, known as apartheid, is wrong. No person should be denied basic rights because of skin color. But does a U.S. Administration have to express its opposition to apartheid by siding with the African National Congress (ANC)? After all, the 1988 booklet entitled *Terrorist Group Profiles*, for which Vice President Bush had written an introductory letter, had called the ANC one of the world's "more notorious terrorist groups."

Mr. Bush was surely aware that the ANC was taken over by the South African Communist Party (SACP) in 1928 and that a U.S. Senate subcommittee revealed at hearings in 1982 that 11 of the 22 members of the ANC's National Executive Committee were also members of the SACP. The head of ANC's military wing, Umkhonto we Sizwe, for many years was Joe Slovo, a Lithuanian-born Communist Party member reputed to be an agent of the Soviet KGB.

But Mr. Bush had nothing but praise for Nelson Mandela, the ANC terrorist leader released from jail in February 1990, and he invited Mandela to visit the White House (see Chapter 2). Mandela had been sent to prison in 1964 for plotting sabotage and the destruction of more than 100 buildings and installations. He had denied that he was a communist, but a manuscript of a booklet found in his possession, in his own handwriting, was entitled *How to Be a Good Communist*. At his trial, he admitted having written a note that said: "We Communist Party members are the most advanced revolutionaries in modern history.... The enemy must be completely crushed and wiped out from the face of the earth before a Communist world can be realized."

Any thoughts that 27 years in jail might have mellowed Mandela were quickly dispelled on the day of his release. Speaking at the Cape Town City Hall on February 11th, he saluted the ANC, saying that "it has fulfilled our every expectation in its role as leader of the great march to freedom.... I salute the South African Communist Party for its steady contribution to the struggle for democracy…. I salute General Secretary Joe Slovo, one of our finest patriots. We are heartened that the alliance between ourselves and the party remains as strong as it has always been."

As for the future, Mandela said, "The factors which necessitated the armed struggle still exist today. We have no option but to continue. We express the hope that a climate conducive to a negotiated settlement would be created soon so that there may no longer be the need for the armed struggle. I am a loyal and disciplined member of the African National Congress. I am, therefore, in full agreement with all of its objectives, strategies, and tactics." He had described the ANC's goals in a letter written a month before: "The nation-alization of the mines, banks, and monopoly industries is the policy of the ANC and a change or modification of our views in this regard is inconceivable…. In our situation, state control of certain sectors of the economy is unavoidable."

In the same letter written from prison, Mandela reiterated his allegiance to the South African Communist Party. He said that "no dedicated ANC member will ever heed a call to break with the SACP. We regard such a demand as a purely divisive government strategy. It is, in fact, a call on us to commit suicide. Which man of honor will ever desert a lifelong friend at the insistence of a common opponent and still retain a measure of credibility among his people?"

Anyone expecting a negative reaction from President Bush to this revolutionary communist battle cry was quickly disappointed. Asked at a news conference on February 12th about Mandela's call for an armed struggle to overturn apartheid, Bush replied: "I read his statement to be more on the defensive side when I looked at it this morning. Yes, we've always advocated nonviolence, and I think the United States ought not to move away from that position."

Asked about Mandela's "rather effusive embrace" of the SACP and the presence of the Communist Party flag on the balcony where he spoke, the President responded: "I didn't notice that. But, you see, I think these communist parties are for the most part sliding downhill. And I think what's coming uphill, and triumphantly so, is democracy and freedom."

Asked what he would do if Mandela "persists in allying himself with a Communist Party," Mr. Bush answered: "Too hypothetical. I mean what's good is that he's out there; he's been in jail a long time.... I'm not embracing every position of the ANC or some of the positions that are represented here today as Mr. Mandela's positions. What I'm doing is embracing the concept that it's good that he's out of jail and that it's good that the South Africans seem to be moving towards a more equitable society."

What South Africa is moving towards, thanks to the Mandelas and Slovos, is an ANC-ruled Marxist-Leninist state aligned with the Soviet Union. Opponents of the ANC can expect to be "necklaced" — a gruesome torture in which the usually black victim is bound (or has his or her hands chopped off) to prevent a struggle and then has an automobile tire placed over his or her head. The tire is soaked with gasoline or diesel fuel and then ignited, causing unbearable agony and slow death for the victim.

One enthusiast for this barbaric practice is Winnie Mandela, Nelson's second wife, who declared in 1986: "We have no arms, but we have stones. We have our boxes of matches. We have our bottles.... With our necklaces, we will liberate this country!" Mrs. Mandela was asked about this statement on the *Donahue* show during her visit to the United States on June 25, 1990. She replied that the words were quoted "completely out of context." That was a lie, and there are videotapes, available from Reed Irvine of Accuracy in Media and Donald McAlvany, that show Mrs. Mandela shouting those exact words at a large outdoor rally in Soweto, South Africa, in April 1986.

Winnie Mandela also had a group of bodyguards, one

of whom was found guilty in May 1990 of murdering a 14-year-old boy who along with three other teenagers had been abducted and savagely beaten in her home in December 1988. Mrs. Mandela was not a defendant in the first trial, even though she had participated in the initial beating of the youths, but she was indicted in September 1990 on four counts of kidnapping and assault. The three surviving teenagers had testified in court that Winnie had started the beatings, hitting 14-year-old "Stompie" Seipei with a stiff whip called a sjambok and urging the other goons to hit him. Stompie's battered body, his throat cut, was found in a field eight days later.

Meanwhile, Nelson Mandela continued to make clear his sympathies for communists. There was a picture on the front page of the April 30, 1990 *New York Times* showing Mandela welcoming Joe Slovo back to South Africa. Both were brandishing the clenched-fist salute identified with the communists since the 1930s. Mandela visited the communist rulers of Angola in May and told them that Cuba was a poor country economically, but "there's one thing where that country stands out head and shoulders above the rest — that is in its love for human rights and liberty."

But nothing Mandela said or did, including his outrageous praise for Fidel Castro, Yasir Arafat, and Muammar Qaddafi during his visit to the United States, seemed to make any difference in the way President Bush treated him. Having already extolled mass murderer Gorbachev, it was certainly not out of character for Mr. Bush to glorify terrorist Mandela.

In a related matter, the Bush Administration also hailed the independence of Namibia, the territory ruled by South Africa for 75 years and turned over in March 1990 to communist Sam Nujoma, the leader of the terrorist South-West Africa People's Organization (SWAPO). "The independence of Nambia today marks the end of colonialism in Africa and a proud beginning for the world's newest country," said President Bush on March 21st. He said that he had sent Secretary of State Baker to the ceremonies in Windhoek "as a sign of the respect and esteem in which we hold the world's newest democracy."

The so-called colonialism of the British, French, Portuguese, and others may have ended with the independence of Namibia, but the colonialism of the Soviet Union continued in countries like Angola, Ethiopia, Mozambique, and Zimbabwe. Americans ought to be asking why the Bush Administration consistently favors liberation movements that enslave rather than liberation movements that liberate.

Iraq

On August 2, 1990, Iraqi dictator Saddam Hussein invaded and seized control of the tiny, oil-rich kingdom of Kuwait and reportedly threatened neighboring Saudi Arabia, one of the world's major suppliers of oil. Calling the invasion an act of "naked aggression," President Bush at first ordered economic sanctions against Iraq and then obtained United Nations approval for stationing U.S. naval forces in the Persian Gulf. By the middle of October, however, he had sent or promised to send more than 300,000 U.S. soldiers, sailors, and Marines to the region in the largest deployment of American military personnel since the Vietnam War. He had also called up tens of thousands of military reservists to supplement the personnel sent to the Middle East.

On September 9th, Mr. Bush had met in Helsinki, Finland, with Soviet ruler Mikhail Gorbachev, and they jointly declared that Iraq's aggression must not be tolerated, saying that "no peaceful international order is possible if larger states can devour their smaller neighbors." It's too bad that the President did not hold Gorbachev to that same standard regarding Estonia, Latvia, and Lithuania.

Mr. Bush asked Gorbachev to withdraw the thousands of Soviet military specialists who had been sent to Iraq to help operate and service the more than $23 billion in military equipment that the USSR had sold to Iraq between 1982 and 1989. But the Kremlin boss refused that request, claiming that there were only 150 or so Soviet specialists in the country and that they would leave when their contracts with the Iraqi government were completed. President Bush said that Gorbachev's refusal was "not a major irritant" and that his Administration was considering economic assistance to the USSR.

Addressing a joint session of Congress on September 11th, the President stated his objectives in the Persian Gulf:

• Iraq must withdraw from Kuwait completely, immediately, and without condition.

• Kuwait's legitimate government must be restored.

• The security and stability of the Persian Gulf must be assured.

• American citizens abroad must be protected....

• Out of these troubled times our fifth objective — a new world order — can emerge: a new era, freer from the threat of terror, stronger in the pursuit of justice, and more secure in the quest for peace.

Of the five stated objectives, only one — the protection of American citizens held in Iraq and Kuwait — was a legitimate reason for putting over 300,000 Americans in harm's way in the Middle East. The President had no constitutional authority to use the armed forces of the United States to settle a dispute between two foreign nations, to guarantee stability in the Persian Gulf, to assure the flow of oil to energy-dependent countries, or to bring about a new world order. America is not the world's policeman, and its military should be used only to protect U.S. territory or to guarantee the safety of American citizens.

The U.S. response to a crisis anywhere in the world should

be to use American forces to obtain the release of any American hostages — and then bring the troops home. U.S. foreign policy should be based on the best interests of a sovereign United States of America and should not be subject to the dictates of the United Nations, NATO, other political or military alliances, or any foreign country.

But that is not the policy George Bush has in mind. He told Congress on September 11th that "our involvement in the gulf is not transitory. It predated Saddam Hussein's aggression and will survive it. Long after all our troops come home, and we all hope it's soon, there will be a lasting role for the United States in assisting the nations of the Persian Gulf. Our role, with others, is to help our friends in their own self-defense. And something else: to curb the proliferation of chemical, biological, ballistic missile, and, above all, nuclear technologies."

On the same day, White House spokesman Marlin Fitzwater confirmed that Mr. Bush had told Mikhail Gorbachev in Helsinki that the Soviet Union would no longer be considered a foe but rather a partner of the United States in the Middle East. "What we're saying now," according to Fitzwater, "is that as this new world order is formed, as we see new cooperation between East and West, between the United States and the Soviet Union in solving regional conflicts, that we believe we should be cooperating with the Soviet Union in the Middle East."

President Bush's penchant for interventionism apparently knows no bounds. It could ultimately sacrifice the sovereignty of the United States on the altar of a new world order.

James Baker endorsed a
Soviet plan to invade
strife-torn Romania.

A.P./Wide World Photos

Nicolae Ceausescu was
executed after 24 years of
cruelty to Romanians.

David Funderburk spent
1981 to 1985 as
America's Ambassador
to Romania.

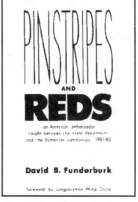

Funderburk's book shows
bankruptcy of the
Reagan-Bush policy
on Romania.

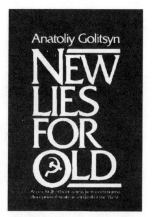

Soviet dictator Stalin
deported or killed
thousands in the
Baltic states.

Anatoliy Golitysn's 1984
book forecast startling
changes in Red Europe.

Anatoliy Golitysn predicted in *New Lies for Old* that
"demolition of the Berlin Wall might even be
contemplated" as part of a false liberalization.

Lech Walesa has said he would "take what's good from socialism."

Daniel Ortega hoped to "rule from below" after losing to Mrs. Chamorro.

President Bush failed to confront Mikhail Gorbachev at Malta about known Soviet military aid to the communists in Nicaragua and El Salvador.

Chapter 6
The Accommodationist

> *Freedom is not a privilege — it is a human right.*
> *The United States has always condemned the violation*
> *of your national sovereignty, and in the years ahead it*
> *will never condone the forced occupation of Lithuania*
> *by the Soviet Union. To do so would be to turn our backs*
> *on our own values and heritage.*
>
> — George Bush to a Lithuanian supporter on
> October 13, 1988,
> as quoted in *Human Events*, May 19, 1990

Republican Presidents in recent decades have gotten away with accommodating communist tryrants in a way that no Democrat could have. Dwight Eisenhower rolled out the red carpet for Nikita Khrushchev just three years after the "Butcher of Budapest" had dispatched his thugs to crush the Hungarian people's quest for freedom. Richard Nixon established ties with a Chinese communist regime that had murdered more of its people than any regime in history. Ronald Reagan initiated a lovefest with Mikhail Gorbachev while the Soviet ruler's army was still slaughtering men, women, and children in Afghanistan.

The question that must be addressed is: How were Republican chief executives able to carry out policies that would have engendered calls for the impeachment of a Democrat who tried the same thing? Much of the answer lies in the public perception that Eisenhower, Nixon, and Reagan were solidly anti-communist in their attitudes and could be trusted not to give away the store in their dealings with Red rulers.

Part of the answer lies too in the fact that expected objections to those policies from anti-communist Republicans were blunted in the interests of party loyalty.

In any case, the public perception was not the reality. While Messrs. Eisenhower, Nixon, and Reagan often sounded anti-communist, and sometimes acted that way too, their policies more often than not advanced the cause of communism and retarded the cause of freedom. Even President Reagan's defeat of the Reds in Grenada was more than offset by his failure to deal effectively with communist governments in Cuba and Nicaragua and by his fawning over Gorbachev.

That same pattern has continued under President Bush, who was willing to abandon the long-suffering people of Lithuania in order to support Gorbachev's perestroika and sign a variety of U.S.-USSR arms control and trade agreements at the June 1990 summit in Washington. Instead of pressuring the Kremlin boss to dismantle his evil empire as a condition for U.S. friendship, Mr. Bush accommodated Gorbachev's desperate need for American aid and trade at the very time that the Soviet ruler was strangling Lithuania economically. This near-frantic pursuit of accommodation on George Bush's part can also be seen regarding Afghanistan, sales of high-technology products to the USSR, and arms control accords that will effectively control only the United States while leaving the liars and cheaters in the Soviet Union free to modernize their arsenal of strategic weapons.

Lithuania

As part of a pact signed with Hitler, the Soviet Union gobbled up Lithuania and the other Baltic states of Estonia and Latvia in the summer of 1940. Stalin's troops immediately killed or deported to slave labor camps near the Arctic Circle tens of thousands, particularly the most influential political, military, business, church, and labor leaders in the three countries. Puppet governments were set up, phony "elections" were held, businesses were seized, all transportation facilities and industries were nationalized, churches were subjected to atheistic regulations, monasteries were closed, schools were placed under Soviet directors, and newspapers were either suppressed or heavily censored.

In June 1941, Hitler turned on his ally Stalin and launched his invasion of the Soviet Union, capturing the Baltic states and ruthlessly dominating them for the next three years. At first, the bitterly anti-communist people of the three small nations joined with the Nazis in fighting their Soviet oppressors, but the Nazi deportation of more thousands of Lithuanians, Estonians, and Latvians to slave labor camps in Germany and the annihilation of half a million Baltic Jews soon made the people bitterly anti-Nazi as well. When the tide of the war turned in 1944, the advancing Soviet army overran the three countries again and, by the end of that year, the Baltic states were absorbed once more into the Soviet Union's slave empire.

It is pertinent to note that the United States never recognized the Soviet takeover of Lithuania. For 50 years, the United States had promised the Lithuanian people that our nation would stand by them if and when they had a chance to regain their independence.

The USSR was still dominating Lithuania in 1990 when the startling changes in communist Europe and all the talk about perestroika prompted the Lithuanians to declare their independence from Moscow on March 11th. Gorbachev immediately called the action "illegal and invalid" and issued a decree ordering the Lithuanians to turn in their firearms (mostly hunting rifles). He next sent tanks rumbling through the capital city of Vilnius, ordered all foreign diplomats and journalists to leave the country, dispatched Soviet soldiers to arrest and beat Lithuanians who had left the Soviet army after the declaration of independence, and warned that any attempts to redraw the USSR's internal borders would lead to "such bloody carnage that we won't be able to crawl out of it."

On April 3rd, the Supreme Soviet passed a Gorbachev-sponsored law requiring republics wishing to secede from the Soviet Union to obtain two-thirds approval from their people in a referendum; setting a five-year transition period for settlement of property and financial questions; and mandating the payment of expenses for all those opposed to independence who wished to leave the country. The law also gave Gorbachev power to declare a state of emergency, permitting him to confiscate firearms, ban rallies and strikes, censor the media, and suspend political activities. Then, on April 17th, Gorbachev stepped up the pressure against Lithuanian independence by ordering a cutoff of oil and natural gas supplies to the Baltic nation's three million people. Lithuania was getting all of its oil and 80 percent of its natural gas from the USSR.

But instead of siding with a people seeking liberty, President Bush said that he did not want to "do something that compels the Soviet Union to take action that would set back the cause of freedom around the world." That policy statement, which Senator Gordon Humphrey called "callous and unfeeling in the extreme," prompted Lithuanian President Vytautas Landsbergis to ask: "Can the freedom of one group of people be sold for the freedom of another? What then is the idea of freedom itself? This is another Munich."

U.S. abandonment of Lithuania had been signaled at least two months earlier by Secretary of State Baker. In February, according to William Safire of the *New York Times*, Baker had ordered the Voice of America to say nothing about Lithuania. He had also ordered VOA editorialists chastised for a February 15th commentary that said:

> Lasting change can come to the Soviet Union when citizens no longer need to fear massive surveillance — and worse — from the KGB. Secret police are also

entrenched in other countries, such as China, North Korea, Iran, Iraq, Syria, Libya, Cuba, and Albania. The rulers of these countries hold power by force and fear, not by the consent of the governed. But as East Europeans demonstrated so dramatically in 1989, the tide of history is against such rulers. The 1990s should belong not to the dictators and secret police, but to the people.

When Mr. Baker was in Namibia in March, according to Latvian-American journalist Juris Kaza, he told Soviet Foreign Minister Eduard Shevardnadze that the Bush Administration supported Soviet plans to draft laws governing how a republic could secede from the USSR. Baker also said that those plans should apply to Lithuania. When Senator Dennis DeConcini (D-AZ) criticized the Administration's policy toward Lithuania, Baker told him: "I think the President, frankly, is in a better position to judge what might or might not be effective for the long run."

Patrick Buchanan, as he often does, put the controversy in its proper perspective in one of his syndicated columns in April:

> The actions of Gorbachev since assuming power are not consistent with those of a democrat in commissar's clothing; they are the acts one would expect of a pan-Slavic, Soviet nationalist who is a devoted follower of Lenin.
>
> To stand with Lithuania is not to demand a new cold war. It is to declare ourselves unwilling to settle for another fake "detente."
>
> True peace can come only when a regime rises in Moscow that looks to Russian national interests, when the constituent republics of the Soviet Union, especially those with ties to the West, are permitted self-determination. With such a regime, we would not need

the false smiles of phony summits or the synthetic security of arms control. At such a Russia there would be no need to point missiles. Gorbachev's conduct of the last few weeks has demonstrated we do not now have that regime.

Finally, on June 29, 1990, the Lithuanian Parliament bowed to the pressure from the United States and the USSR and agreed to suspend its declaration of independence from the Soviet Union for 100 days and enter into negotiations with the Kremlin rulers. Gorbachev responded by ordering resumption of oil, gas, and food deliveries to Lithuania. The sanctions imposed after the March 11th declaration had put an estimated 40,000 Lithuanians out of work, and the government in Vilnius could no longer stand on principle while its people were hurting economically and its alleged allies in Washington were siding with the Soviet oppressors.

Afghanistan

During a visit to a refugee camp at the Khyber Pass near the border between Afghanistan and Pakistan on May17, 1984, Vice President Bush condemned the "brutal Soviet invasion and continuing war against Afghanistan" and told the Afghan freedom fighters, "Your cause is just.… You are not alone. Long live Afghanistan." Five years later, the world thought the war was over following the withdrawal of more than 100,000 Soviet troops after a decade-long occupation that had killed nearly three million Afghans, made refugees out of another six million, and devastated a land in which there had been only 15 million people when the Soviet army invaded in 1979.

Close observers of the scene were not as optimistic, however. Not only had the departing Soviet forces sowed the countryside with more than 30 million mines to prevent the refugees from returning home, but they had also left behind more than $1 billion worth of military equipment, supplies, and installations. In the last half of 1989, said Roseanne Klass of Freedom House, the regime in Kabul led by Soviet puppet Najibullah had been provided with "a new professional Afghan army created inside the USSR, nearly a thousand SCUD missiles, hundreds of tanks (including an entire T-72M brigade), self-propelled artillery and rocket launchers, FROG-7B missiles, and MiG-29s and Sukhoi SU-27s, the latter a plane so advanced that it has never before been based outside the Soviet Union (and for which no non-Soviet pilots are known to have been trained)."

The new professional Afghan army created inside the USSR was drawn from the tens of thousands of Afghan children abducted and taken to Moscow in the early 1980s and returned to Afghanistan as trained military and security personnel. In addition, over 500 Soviet military personnel were known to be in Afghanistan as of May 1990, and Gorbachev was providing $500 million a month in weapons and other war materiel.

Isabel Rivero-Arguelles, a journalist and volunteer for the Free Afghanistan Alliance, has been in and out of the ravaged country since 1987. Reporting in the spring of 1990 about her recent five-month stretch of "combat duty" there, she noted "the heroism of the freedom fighters as well as the horrors still wrought among the civilian population by Soviet weapons like the 'Uragon' missile." Read her chilling account of one such attack:

> One night I was caught in an attack by six guided "Uragon" missiles. It was as if you were caught in an earthquake, with the ground heaving and buckling, the sound as of four freight trains on a collision course; mortar in buildings turning into powder and the glass in window frames shattering as if by the blows of invisible hammers instead of flying out as it does during the

usual bombing raids. Each "Uragon" has a fragmentation mechanism with 40 to 50 separate explosions. When buildings are hit, the destruction is almost total and the wounds are awful.

While the Soviet assault on Afghanistan continued, U.S. aid to the freedom fighters was reduced almost to nothing and then resumed on a small and sporadic basis. The Bush Administration had originally insisted on the ouster of Soviet stooge Najibullah before beginning negotiations for a transitional government. But at talks in Moscow in February 1990, Secretary of State Baker said that the Administration was willing to drop its demand that Najibullah be removed before any negotiated settlement. This move toward a final sellout of the brave Afghan people was immediately denounced by a group of Senators, including Robert Byrd (D-WV) and Bob Dole (R-KS), in a letter to Secretary Baker:

> The endorsement of any so-called "transitional" government which includes Najibullah and/or his close associates would put the United States into the unconscionable position of legitimizing a regime which presided over the brutalization of the Afghan people and the destruction of the very fabric of their society over a decade of killing and armed occupation.

Having already legitimized other brutal communist regimes, such as Red China, why should the Senators expect anything different from the Bush Administration with regard to Afghanistan? Mr. Bush's nice-sounding words — "You are not alone" — were only words.

High-Technology Sales

In an interview with *Conservative Digest* in January 1986, Vice President Bush called for stronger controls "to prevent the export of strategic Free World technology to communist countries." He said that "there is an enormous amount of espionage. We had a nonclassified white paper the other day that really deserves wide circulation. That paper covered the acquisition of our high technology by the Soviet Union. It is a very frightening document, and I sent copies to many businesspeople around this country to show them what we are up against."

Three years later, with Mr. Bush now in the White House, the Defense Department's publication *Soviet Military Power: Prospects for Change* expressed the same concerns. "The Soviets are exploiting improved relations with the West to implement cooperative science and technology programs and exchanges," the report said. "The resulting technology transfer from these activities provides significant benefits to the Soviet defense industry.... The long-running Soviet program of legal and illegal acquisition of foreign technology has not diminished. This program, coupled with the pursuit of technology through joint ventures and exchanges, is vital to the Soviets' strategy of upgrading their competitiveness in military technology."

Why, then, would George Bush act contrary to his own concerns and the Defense Department's very sensible views early in his Presidency? First, his Commerce Department approved the export of computers to the Soviet bloc. With enhanced capabilities, those computers had double the performance level of previous models cleared for export. Next, it was a broad range of desktop personal computers which had supposedly become available from other countries. Secretary of Commerce Robert Mosbacher said that approval was part of the President's plan to "improve prospects for prosperity for Eastern Europe without harming America's national security." But Secretary of Defense Dick Cheney objected, saying that "raising the level of sophistication of those computers sold to the Soviet Union or East bloc countries ... would give them significant capabilities that they do not now possess. The technology in those computers is not generally available."

By March of 1990, however, Cheney had dropped his opposition to such sales and, on May 2nd, the Administration proposed relaxing curbs on the export of advanced computers, precision machine tools, and telecommunications equipment to the Reds. Asked at a news conference the following day about the easing of those controls, especially while the USSR was cracking down on Lithuania, President Bush replied: "What we're doing is putting up tighter walls around needed items that are in the national security interest.... And I don't view this as giving something to the Soviets at all."

That "logic" escaped former Pentagon official Frank Gaffney, who said that by decontrolling 43 militarily relevant technologies, "the Administration is permitting the Soviet Union to obtain highly capable computers, sophisticated machine tools, and a variety of telecommunications, electronic, and other technologies previously denied lest they be applied to Soviet defense purposes." In Gaffney's view, the decontrol would:

(1) "greatly facilitate the Soviet military's effort to develop and manufacture its next generation of advanced weapons systems,"

(2) enable the Kremlin "to maintain a threatening state-of-the-art defense establishment at substantially lower cost,"

(3) "seriously erode the qualitative edge upon which U.S. and allied security has traditionally depended," permitting the USSR "to counter advanced American weapon systems far more effectively," and

(4) "add significantly to the costs involved in preserving the United States' technological advantage in decisive military areas like anti-submarine warfare,

low observable aircraft, and precision munitions."

Gaffney may have been thinking about Toshiba's sale to the Soviet Union of machine tools that would make quieter propellers for submarines. That technology cost the USSR only $18 million, but it was expected to cost the United States an estimated $10 billion to overcome its weakened anti-sub warfare capabilities.

In addition to high-tech sales, the Bush Administration was busily aiding the Kremlin in several other remarkable ways: implementing what Secretary of State Baker called "a program of extensive technical cooperation with the Soviets designed to facilitate the massive task of restructuring their economy"; authorizing reciprocal visits in 1989 by Joint Chiefs of Staff Chairman Admiral William J. Crowe and Soviet military chief of staff Marshal Sergei Akhromeyev, leading possibly to an exchange of "parties of soldiers," according to Soviet Defense Minister Dmitri Yazov; promoting joint ventures in the Soviet Union by American companies; and arranging increased sales of American grain to the USSR.

The General Accounting Office reported in March 1990 that the U.S. taxpayers had coughed up $481 million over the previous 29 months to subsidize wheat sales to the Soviet Union, and $299.5 million during the same period for subsidized wheat sales to Communist China. The subsidies went to U.S. export companies that ship wheat to the Reds at less-than-market prices. It was bad enough selling wheat to tyrannical regimes, but selling it at bargain-basement prices and taxing the American people to pay the difference was even worse. Accommodation of the communists knows no bounds.

Lenin was right when he predicted in the 1920s:

> The capitalists of the world and their governments,
> in pursuit of conquest of the Soviet market, will close

their eyes to the indicated higher reality and thus will turn into deaf mute blindmen. They will extend credits, which will strengthen for us the Communist Party in their countries and, giving us the materials and technology we lack, they will restore our military industry, indispensable for our future victorious attacks on our suppliers. In other words, they will labor for the preparation for their own suicide.

What makes U.S. aid to the Kremlin so crazy is that the Soviet Union is continuing to devote enormous amounts of its budget to modernizing and increasing the size of its military arsenal. Contrary to reports of cutbacks in Soviet military spending, the Gorbachev regime is still producing each year twice the number of tanks and 10 times the artillery of all the NATO countries combined, according to the International Security Council (ISC). Citing an April 1990 Defense Intelligence Agency report to Congress, the privately run ISC said that the Pentagon agency's findings included these:

Huge stockpiles of Soviet arms remain in Eastern Europe and are being increasingly updated; there has been no slowdown in naval force modernization; vigorous and broadly based modernization of both strategic offensive and defensive forces continues, with very high rates of production; conversion of military plants to civilian industry remains virtually nonexistent; "no major weapons development program appears to have been stretched out or cancelled"; and the Soviets continue to deliver $17 billion a year in military support to their Third World clients (interestingly enough, about the level of the proposed Western aid package to the Soviet Union).

The Bush Administration's policy toward the communists

should be a total boycott — no aid, trade, "cultural exchanges," or any kind of assistance that would help them achieve their goals. (Gorbachev said in 1987, "We are moving toward a new world, the world of communism. We shall never turn off that road.") The Free World has sustained its most dangerous enemy for more than 70 years. It is past time to reverse that suicidal policy. "The Soviets are depending on us to continue to supply them with 'the rope' until they have enough to hang us," Senator William Armstrong has said. "But there is still time to yank the rope away."

Arms Control

In his State of the Union message on January 31, 1990, President Bush said, "We recognize that the Soviet military threat is diminishing, but we see little change in Soviet strategic modernization. Therefore, we must sustain our own strategic offense modernization and the Strategic Defense Initiative." Secretary of State Baker went to Moscow a few months later and reported that his discussions with Soviet officials had resulted in "some real accomplishments," particularly in arms control. Aides to Baker told reporters that when disputes arose over such matters as how many bombers should be allowed to carry cruise missiles, or how many sea-launched cruise missiles should be permitted, the Secretary and Mikhail Gorbachev agreed to "split the difference."

But in his May 21st column in the *New York Times*, William Safire charged that Baker had actually "caved in to basic Gorbachev demands all the way down the line." He said that Baker failed to get a Soviet commitment to end its military occupation of Central and Eastern Europe; let Gorbachev retain the right to modernize his SS-18 missiles (154 of the improved SS-18s will be more powerful than the 304 in existence at the time), while giving up the U.S. right to improve its cruise missiles; went along with Gorbachev's refusal to allow on-site verification of Soviet missile production facilities; and obtained no limits on the long-range Soviet Backfire bomber, several hundred of which were already deployed, with 30 more being added each year.

Regarding the range of U.S. air-launched cruise missiles, Safire said: "We originally wanted 1,500 kilometers, to be able to penetrate the Soviet Union if the Red Army attacked Europe; they said 600. We dickered downward; they said 600. The Baker 'split difference': 600." That concession was so favorable to the USSR, said Richard Perle, an Assistant Secretary of Defense in the Reagan Administration, that "it was resisted by administrations for 20 years."

Asked about Safire's charges, the Secretary of State denied them, saying that "it's been pretty much all the other way around.... In terms of what we have given and what we have taken, we have done very well indeed." The Baker-Gorbachev negotiations were codified in agreements signed by Bush and Gorbachev at their Washington summit meeting in June 1990.

Those agreements have no more chance of being honestly adhered to by the USSR than any of the other arms accords its rulers have signed with the United States, and then violated repeatedly. Take, for one example, the Intermediate Range Nuclear Forces Treaty (INF) of 1987. Appearing on the PBS *Firing Line* program in October 1987, Vice President Bush defended that treaty as "the first time in the nuclear age that we are getting rid of a whole class of nuclear weapons, and that's good for my grandchildren and the rest of the world."

But it's only good if the Soviet Union honors the treaty, which it has not. In March 1989, the Bush Administration discovered that the USSR had secretly transferred at least 24 SS-23 mobile missiles to communist East Germany, a clear violation of the INF treaty. A year later, Soviet personnel at the Votkinsk missile factory breached the INF treaty three times during the weekend of March 9-10, 1990; they refused

U.S. inspectors their right under a treaty provision to use an x-ray device to monitor cannisters leaving the factory to make sure that the SS-20 missiles banned by the treaty were no longer being assembled at the facility.

The Soviets not only blocked the U.S. monitoring effort on March 9th, said a report from Frank Gaffney's Center for Security Policy, "they actually rammed a locomotive towing a missile railcar through the U.S. treaty monitoring station without stopping for the mandated inspections. This action was repeated on March 10th with two more railcars bearing missile cannisters. In the process of crashing through the U.S. portal-monitoring facility, the Soviets reportedly damaged a barrier and warning device."

On May 17th of that year, Senator James McClure (R-ID) offered an amendment on the Senate floor to condemn the Soviet Union "for its willful act denying our treaty right to image the three Soviet missiles which exited the facility at Votkinsk on March 9-10, 1990." The McClure amendment was rejected by a vote of 56 to 39.

Is President Bush aware of these treaty violations? Of course he is. On February 23, 1990, he submitted to Congress, as required by law, a report on "Soviet Noncompliance with Arms Control Agreements." The report, said Mr. Bush, "addresses issues of Soviet failure to comply with existing arms control agreements, including the 1987 Intermediate Range Nuclear Forces Treaty (INF) and the 1972 Anti-Ballistic Missile (ABM) Treaty. The 1974 Threshold Test Ban Treaty (TTBT), the 1963 Limited Test Ban Treaty (LTBT), the Biological and Toxin Weapons Convention (BWC), and the Geneva Protocol on Chemical Weapons are treated later in this section of the report."

Despite this abysmal record of arms treaty violations by Soviet rulers going back to 1963, Mr. Bush said in his February report that "my Administration is committed to the pursuit of new arms control agreements that reduce the threat of the outbreak of war and contribute to international stability." Four months later, he agreed to sign more arms accords with Gorbachev. Americans concerned about the security of the United States have good reason to question President Bush's commitment to protecting that security when he is so willing to sign agreements with history's most notorious treaty-breakers.

Bush and the KGB

Another indication of George Bush's accommodationist attitude was an incredible statement he made in 1982 about the KGB, the fearsome Soviet secret police apparatus whose half a million agents engage in mass repression of the people within the USSR while conducting espionage, terrorism, and assassinations abroad. Referring to the new Soviet ruler Yuri Andropov, who had presided over the KGB for 15 years, Mr. Bush said: "My view of Andropov is that some people make this KGB thing sound horrendous. Maybe I speak defensively as a former head of the CIA. But leave out the operational side of the KGB — the naughty things they allegedly do — here's a man who's had access to a tremendous amount of intelligence over the years."

The "naughty things they allegedly do"! A vastly different picture of this Soviet Gestapo can be found in the books of John Barron (*KGB* and *KGB Today*) and Stanislav Levchenko (*On the Wrong Side: My Life in the KGB* and, with Herbert Romerstein, *The KGB Against the "Main Enemy"*). Oleg Gordievsky, a former KGB station chief in London who defected to the West in 1985, told *Time* magazine in March 1990 that the KGB brought Gorbachev to power and "remains an important tool for him." Gordievsky also said that the KGB was continuing its "massive internal espionage" and its "huge network of intelligence stations" in foreign countries, with at least 100 agents in Washington and at least another 100 in New York City.

Gorbachev's man at the helm of the KGB in 1990 was Vladimir Kryuchkov, who told the Supreme Soviet on July 14, 1989, that for KGB officers, "peacetime, as far as they are concerned, is combat time." And U.S. intelligence officials were reporting in 1990 that Soviet espionage operations to steal American technology had increased as Gorbachev was promoting his phony glasnost and perestroika.

Kryuchkov "was for many, many years chief of foreign contacts, the International Department of the KGB, the part of the KGB which works in the West to destroy you," said Avraham Shifrin, a former prisoner in the Soviet gulag now living in Israel. "Kryuchkov was responsible for this work for many years. Now he is the head of the KGB. It means very much. It shows very much."

What it shows is that there are no accommodationists in the Politburo or in the KGB, but there certainly are some in Washington, DC.

Panama's Manuel Noriega
was deposed by President
Bush's action.

Terrorist Nelson Mandela
gives the clenched-fist
salute favored
by communists.

"Necklacing" is the terrible torture inflicted by
the African National Congress on black South Africans
who oppose its Marxism-Leninism.

President Bush meets in Saudi Arabia with
Kuwait's leader, Sheik Jaber Al-Sabah, during his
November 1990 trip to the Middle East.

Members of the Third Marine Regiment on
station in the Saudi desert near the Iraq border.
An amphibious assault vehicle is shown.

Columnist Pat Buchanan scored President Bush for abandoning Lithuania.

Senator James McClure denounced the USSR for arms treaty violations.

Lenin was right when he predicted that capitalists would commit suicide.

Michail Makarenko said President Bush must stop legitimizing Gorbachev.

Chapter 7
The Perestroikaist

> *I will tell President Gorbachev, the dynamic archi-*
> *tect of Soviet reform, that America wants the people of*
> *the Soviet Union to fulfill their destiny. And I will assure*
> *him that there is no greater advocate of perestroika*
> *than the President of the United States.*
>
> — George Bush in his Thanksgiving message
> to the American people, November 22, 1989

Ever since Franklin D. Roosevelt referred to Stalin as "Uncle Joe," American Presidents have tried to gloss over the evil nature of the Hitler-like rulers in the Kremlin. They have done so despite mountains of evidence — and tens of millions of corpses — that gave the lie to their image-making efforts. For whatever reason, each President felt compelled to succeed where his predecessors had failed.

But it was the Soviet rulers, and not the American leaders, who came out on top when Roosevelt and Truman met with Stalin, when Eisenhower and Kennedy met with Khrushchev, when Johnson met with Kosygin, when Nixon, Ford, and Carter met with Brezhnev, and when Reagan and Bush met with Gorbachev. Reagan was the only chief executive who resisted the summit compulsion at first, and he even correctly described the USSR as the "evil empire." But he too eventually succumbed to the siren song of summitry and told the American people that the Red leopard had changed its spots.

Not since FDR, however, has any President slopped over a Soviet slavemaster the way George Bush has gushed over Gorbachev, although Mr. Bush will play the "bad-cop" role once in a while. On February 6, 1990, in a classic case of telling an audience what it wanted to hear, he told U.S. troops at Fort Irwin, California: "It is important not to let these encouraging changes [in the Soviet bloc] — political or military — lull us into a sense of complacency. Nor can we let down our guard against a worldwide threat. The Soviet Union still maintains formidable forces. Military challenges to democracy persist in every hemisphere." But otherwise the President has become one of Gorbachev's most ardent promoters. Some examples follow.

Bush on Gorbachev

• December 1989 — "There is certainly an element of respect for the way he has managed the change in Eastern Europe and his determination to fight for perestroika reform at home. I have more respect for him than I did when he first came into office, back when I first met him, or when I saw him last year."

• January 1990 — "He's different from his predecessors.... He talks about democratic values. How many of the other Soviet leaders have ever discussed that? He's talking about openness, which we all agree with, glasnost, freedom to choose in elections, the right of countries to self-determine, all the things we believe. And not only is he talking about it, but in the way he's acting in Eastern Europe, why he seems to be encouraging it.... He is identified, as nobody else in the world today, with moving things toward democratic values and moving things toward a more peaceful world."

• January 1990 — "I want very much for him to succeed. I think he has conducted himself in an extraordinarily difficult situation very well. He remains committed to peaceful change. And I don't think anyone is faulting him for the difficulties that he has encountered in Azerbaijan." Asked about Gorbachev's use of force to put down demonstrations in Azerbaijan, Bush replied: "You see blockades of your ports, and the man has to respond. I'm not encouraging that course because we would like to see peaceful change wherever possible.... But as I look around, I think Mr. Gorbachev is really the best hope for what our interests are."

• May 1990 — "We've seen a world of change this past year.... Mr. President, you deserve great credit for your part in these transforming events. I salute you, as well, for the process of change you've brought to your own country.... We know about the difficult economic reforms that are necessary to breathe new vigor into the Soviet economy. And as I've said many times before, we want to see perestroika succeed."

• June 1990 — "Let me say how productive I really feel the last few days have been. President Gorbachev and I have agreed to meet on a regular basis, perhaps annually. Both of us would like to think that we can get together more often with less formality. Because, you see, we're now at a stage in the U.S.-Soviet relationship, and indeed in world history, where we should miss no opportunity to complete the extraordinary tasks before us. Mr. President, it's been a pleasure having you here, Sir."

The ongoing political canonization of Gorbachev was accompanied by the silencing of Administration officials who suggested a more cautious assessment and by the ignoring of actions that contradicted the peacemaker image. In October 1989, Secretary of State James Baker barred deputy national security advisor Robert Gates from giving a speech to the National Collegiate Security Conference in Bethesda, Maryland, because it was too pessimistic about Gorbachev's chances of success in reforming the USSR. A year before, Gates, who was then deputy director of the CIA, had said in a speech: "Whether Gorbachev succeeds or fails, or just survives, a still long competition and struggle with the Soviet Union lies before us."

In February 1990, State Department spokeswoman Margaret Tutwiler confirmed that the Soviet Union had recently shipped more Soviet MiG-29s to Castro's regime in Cuba. She said that the Administration could not understand why Gorbachev would send fighter planes to Castro when the Cuban dictator had criticized the Soviet ruler's policies. She noted that Secretary Baker had told the Soviets the plane delivery was something the United States "cannot tolerate." But since nothing had been done about it, one reporter said, "it sounds like we're tolerating it." Tutwiler responded: "Those are your words. I'm going to stick to the Secretary's, which point is not to get hung up on the word tolerate."

Gorbachev the Leninist

Is Mikhail Gorbachev the savior of the Soviet Union and a worthy recipient of the 1990 Nobel Peace Prize? Or is he another dangerous disciple of Lenin, a well-dressed Bolshevik who has carried on a public relations campaign that would be the envy of Madison Avenue? A look at his background, his words, and his actions will give the answer.

Mikhail Sergeyevich Gorbachev was born in Stavropol on March 2, 1931. After becoming a top official of the Young Communist League in Stavropol, he went to Moscow and was graduated from Moscow State University in 1955. While advancing through the ranks of the Communist Party in Stavropol, he got to know Yuri Andropov, an area native who frequently vacationed there while he was heading the KGB.

When the post of Central Committee Secretary of Agriculture became available in 1978, Gorbachev was named to the job. He was promoted to full membership in the Politburo in 1980, acted as point man for General Secretary Andropov's purge of top-ranking communist leaders in 1983, and was elected in 1984 as chairman of the Foreign Affairs Committee of the Supreme Soviet. When Konstantin Chernenko died in 1985, the ruling Politburo chose Gorbachev to be General Secretary of the Communist Party of the Soviet Union.

The new Soviet party boss immediately made clear his intentions by declaring that "we will firmly follow the Leninist course of peace and peaceful coexistence." To the naive, that sounded wonderful; to those who knew that peace, in the communist lexicon, meant that all opposition to communism had been destroyed, it sounded ominous. Furthermore, it was Lenin who said in 1920: "As long as capitalism and socialism exist, we cannot live in peace; in the end, one or the other will triumph — a funeral dirge will be sung over the Soviet Republic or over world capitalism."

Gorbachev has since issued a continuing stream of his own Leninist statements:

   • November 1987 — "In October 1917, we parted with the Old World, rejecting it once and for all. We are moving toward a new world, the world of communism. We shall never turn off that road."

   • November 1987 — "In our work and worries, we are motivated by those Leninist ideals and noble endeavors and goals which mobilized the workers of Russia seven decades ago to fight for the new and happy world of socialism. Perestroika is a continuation of the October Revolution."

   • October 1989 — "The concept, the main idea, lies in the fact that we want to give a new lease on life to socialism through perestroika and to reveal the potential of the socialist system, overcoming people's alienation from property, the means of production, the political process, power and culture. In my opinion, this is essentially a truly Marxist formulation of the problem: it puts people first."

• December 1989 — "I am a communist, a convinced communist. For some that may be a fantasy. But for me it is my main goal."

• April 1990 — To those advisors who wanted him to "let market conditions be put in place everywhere; let's have free enterprise and give the green light to all forms of ownership, private ownership; let everything be private; let us sell the land, everything," Gorbachev said: "I cannot support such ideas, no matter how decisive and revolutionary they might appear. These are irresponsible ideas, irresponsible."

• April 1990 — "The Bolshevik art of convincing the people of one's correctness needs to be revived."

Anyone familiar with the bloody Bolshevik takeover of Russia in 1917 will remember that "the Bolshevik art of convincing the people of one's correctness" resulted in the slaughter of 10 million Russians from 1918 to 1920 before Lenin crushed all major opposition to his policies. Using the dreaded Cheka, the predecessor of the KGB, to conduct a campaign of mass terror and execution against the people, Lenin said that the guillotine used during the French Revolution "only terrorized active resistance.... We have to break down passive resistance, which doubtless is the most harmful and dangerous of all." He said that "we shall be ruthless toward our enemies, as well as toward all hesitant and noxious elements" — thus including virtually the entire population of Russia at that time.

Gorbachev the Stalinist

During his first five years in power, the man President Bush called "the dynamic architect of Soviet reform" directed the massacre of 500,000 Afghan civilians. Because Gorbachev was a member of the ruling Politburo beginning in 1980, he actually shares the guilt for virtually all of the atrocities committed in Afghanistan. He has maintained more than 2,000 labor camps in the USSR with an estimated 10 million prisoners in them, according to former gulag inhabitant Avraham Shifrin who has published maps showing the location of the camps. He has supplied war materiel to his puppets in Afghanistan, Angola, Cuba, Libya, Nicaragua, North Korea, Syria, and elsewhere. And he has continued building and modernizing the Soviet nuclear and strategic arsenal, producing hundreds of submarine-launched and intercontinental ballistic missiles.

While accepting verbal bouquets for his policies of glasnost and perestroika, and promising to bring about a "humane socialism" in the USSR, Gorbachev actually accumulated a wide range of dictatorial powers. The strengthened presidency of the Soviet Union gave him authority to rule by decree, fire top Soviet officials, mobilize the military, and in general control every aspect of life in the country. By April 1990, said CIA chief William Webster, Gorbachev had become "the most powerful leader since Josef Stalin."

In 1989, Gorbachev signed a decree imposing prison sentences of three to ten years for such "crimes" as calling for the overthrow of the Soviet system or for "its alteration in ways contradicting the USSR constitution," which could mean challenging the role of the Communist Party as "the leading and guiding force of Soviet society." His list of "crimes" also included using "technical equipment" to produce materials critical of the regime and inciting "ethnic or racial hostility or strife." After he was jeered by people watching the May Day parade in 1990, he pushed through a law making the insulting of a president a crime punishable by up to six years in prison.

As it has been presented to the Free World, perestroika is a sham. Neither the performance of the economy nor the living standards of the people have improved; in fact, they have actually worsened under Gorbachev. The American standard of living was at least five times higher as of 1990, one-third of Soviet hospitals did not have running water, persons with so-called independent collective farms could only rent them from the state and were regulated by state dictates, and, at the end of 1989, only 50 of the 1,200 standard consumer products in the USSR were freely available for purchase in state stores.

But the key to unlocking the real meaning of perestroika is to understand what Gorbachev himself says it is. In his 1987 book *Perestroika*, he stated: "We are not going to change Soviet power, of course, or abandon its fundamental principles, but we acknowledge the need for changes that will strengthen socialism and make it more dynamic and politically meaningful." If the purpose of perestroika is to strengthen socialism, and if, as Mr. Bush has said, "there is no greater advocate of perestroika than the President of the United States," doesn't that mean that George Bush is in favor of strengthening socialism in the USSR?

"The main elements of the totalitarian society in the Soviet Union remain," Oleg Gordievsky told *Time* magazine in March 1990. "They are the one-party state, the state-owned economy with one acceptable ideology for the whole society, and the secret police." Why have the communists eased some of the restrictions on the people? "Because it is impossible to continue to preserve their power without permitting people some little things, little freedoms," said Michail Makarenko, a prisoner in the gulag for eight years who was allowed to emigrate to the West and founded a group called Resistance International. "But there is no freedom of speech; there is no freedom of the press. That does not exist."

The Soviet Mafia

Michail Makarenko told *The New American* magazine in February 1990 that "the Soviet government is not a legitimate government. The people of our country look upon it as a

Mafia, a gang of criminals." He said that "when your President just shakes the hand of a communist leader, he is giving him aid, assistance. He is legitimizing him by his position in your country.... Stop praising Gorbachev, giving him material assistance — even, for example, the compliments to Gorbachev. I think that they are worth more than the billions and billions of dollars he got in real aid."

It would be nice to think that the changes in the Soviet Union were leading to political and economic freedom for the long-oppressed people in that vast country. But if they were, they would be accompanied by such things as withdrawal of all Soviet troops from other countries, genuine liberation for Central and Eastern Europe and those regions of the USSR that were once independent, termination of all KGB operations, abolition of all labor camps and release of all prisoners of conscience, completely open elections, the abandonment of the corrupt socialist system, and freedom of speech, religion, press, assembly, and so forth.

George Bush knows the meaning of those freedoms. Why hasn't he conditioned U.S. policy toward the Soviet Union on progress toward those goals? Why has he ignored the desperate plight of the Soviet people and chosen instead to keep the Communist Party in power in that land? "Surely," said A.M. Rosenthal in the December 5, 1989 *New York Times*, "Americans never realized the role Mr. Bush selected would be to provide life support for the Soviet Communist Party, keeping it breathing through more years of pain and suffering for the Soviet people."

Mikhail Gorbachev is a dangerous disciple of the USSR's Lenin and Stalin.

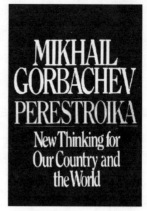

The goal of perestroika, Gorbachev has said, is to "strengthen socialism."

Avraham Shifrin, a former prisoner in the Soviet Gulag Archipelago, has created a map showing the location of slave labor camps in the Soviet Union.

Chapter 8
The Obscurantist

*George Bush is the typical Nixon type: no prin-
ciples, no beliefs, and no moral shame in selling a
policy he once bitterly opposed.*
— Jeffrey St. John, October 20, 1971, as quoted
in *The Review Of The News*, February 6, 1980

Webster's New World Dictionary defines an obscurantist
as a person who is opposed to human progress and enlight-
enment. If the word is applied to his policy on Red China from
1970 to 1990, then George Bush is an obscurantist par
excellence. He had told the people of Texas during his 1964
campaign for the U.S. Senate that "if Red China should be
admitted to the UN, then the UN is hopeless and we should
withdraw." But seven years later, Bush did an about-face and
welcomed Red China to the United Nations, saying that its
presence made the UN "more reflective of the world as it now
exists." Mr. Bush has frequently reversed his positions, and
virtually every reversal has favored either communists abroad
or big government at home.

President Nixon had named George Bush Ambassador to
the UN in December 1970 and, ten months later, the new
ambassador urged the seating of both Red China and Free
China in the General Assembly. The body voted, however, to
admit the communist regime and expel America's allies on
Taiwan. Mr. Bush called the vote a "moment of infamy," but
three weeks later greeted the delegates from mainland China
and expressed the hope that they would "contribute to the organization's potential for harmonizing the actions of nations."

The communist delegate's maiden speech was anything but harmonious as he blasted the presence of U.S. forces in Southeast Asia and said his country was "opposed to the power-politics hegemony of big nations bullying small ones." Ambassador Bush called the speech "a disappointment for all those who wish to see the UN promote its goals of peace and progress," but a week later he welcomed the Chinese Reds to the UN Security Council and said he looked forward to cooperating with them. The Mao Tse-tung regime's permanent envoy again denounced the "one or two superpowers" who were "carrying out aggression, interference, subversion, and control against other countries and their people."

The Human Cost of Communism

Bear in mind that at the same time George Bush was trying to make the Chinese communists seem respectable, the Senate Internal Security Subcommittee was releasing a report entitled *The Human Cost of Communism in China*. The report was the product of the painstaking efforts of Professor Richard L. Walker, a lifelong student of Chinese affairs. After having studied all the evidence, he concluded in the report that communists in China, from the time of the first civil war (1927-1936) until 1971, had killed a minimum of 34 million people and possibly as many as 64 million!

Professor Walker's concluding remarks, which should have been required reading for Ambassador Bush and other members of the Nixon Administration, have proved to be disturbingly accurate:

> If the outside world cannot learn that the Chinese Communist leaders are indeed a remarkable group of "true believers" in their doctrines, if we are prone to forget or ignore their history and their past actions, if we do not exercise the wisdom which can point toward the day when the Chinese people can abandon class struggle

and revolutionary world violence as the path to their modernization, then the human cost of Communism in China, detailed in the pages above, will, in all probability, mount very much higher.

The next phase of George Bush's association with the Chinese Reds, his 14 months as the U.S. envoy in what was then called Peking, started him on his quest to make saints out of history's most murderous sinners. Not the latest atrocities in Beijing, not the regime's barbaric policy of forced abortion, not the most egregious human rights abuses, not the rape of Tibet, not even the repeated insults and arrogant rejections of expressions of concern by the United States could deter Mr. Bush in his quest.

Former FBI Director J. Edgar Hoover once said that a person could learn more about communism by spending 15 days in the library than 15 days in a communist country. A few hours with *The Human Cost of Communism* would have done George Bush more good than 14 months in Red China and his visits there in 1980, 1982, and 1985. That is, if Mr. Bush were not so totally committed to ignoring the Red Chinese regime's crimes against the Chinese people.

Massacre in Tiananmen Square

On June 4, 1989, two weeks after President Bush had encouraged Chinese students and workers demonstrating in Beijing for democratic changes and more freedom to "fight for what you believe in," the communist rulers ordered the army to move into Tiananmen Square and crush the peaceful protesters. Using tanks, armored personnel carriers, and automatic weapons, the Red soldiers slaughtered thousands. They shot people looking on from windows above the square, rolled tanks over the wounded, and burned the bodies of the dead to destroy the evidence. Tens of thousands were arrested and many of them were later executed. Maoism had returned.

At a news conference on June 5th, Mr. Bush deplored the massacre and urged the Red Chinese rulers "to avoid violence and to return to their previous policy of restraint." He said that his Administration could not "ignore the consequences for our relationship with China," and his list of sanctions called for "suspension of all government-to-government sales and commercial exports of weapons, suspension of visits between U.S. and Chinese military leaders, sympathetic review of requests by Chinese students in the United States to extend their stay, the offer of humanitarian and medical assistance through the Red Cross to those injured during the assault, and review of other aspects of our bilateral relationship as events in China continue to unfold."

It was a weak response to a brutal massacre and its weakness was magnified by the President's actions one month later. On July 7th, Secretary of State Baker approved a waiver of sanctions so the Boeing company could sell four commercial jetliners to Red China. And even more astounding, although it was not learned until six months later, Mr. Bush sent the CFR-Kissinger twins, Brent Scowcroft and Lawrence Eagleburger, to Beijing that same month! White House spokesman Marlin Fitzwater would later defend the secret mission, saying that the two high-ranking officials went to "personally underscore the U.S. shock and concern about the violence in Tiananmen Square and to impress upon the Chinese government the seriousness with which this incident was viewed in the United States."

Now remember that the July mission was not revealed until after Scowcroft and Eagleburger returned to Beijing in December 1989. Secretary Baker at first lied about the July trip, saying that the December mission was "the first time we've had high-level United States officials go to the People's Republic of China." On December 19th, the day that Baker admitted he had "misled" the American people about the July visit, President Bush lifted the sanctions to allow the export of three communications satellites to Red China, and to permit the Export-Import Bank to issue loans and guarantees for U.S. exports to the communist mainland. Congress had in November barred such loans unless the President decided that such activity was in the "national interest." Favoring the communist side once again, Mr. Bush said that it was.

Secret Missions to Beijing

Asked at a December 21st news conference why he had kept the Scowcroft-Eagleburger missions secret, Mr. Bush cited his "obligation as President to conduct the foreign policy of this country the way I see fit, reporting under the law to the United States Congress." He defended his actions by insisting: "There's a lot going on that, in the conduct of foreign policy or a debate within the U.S. government, has to be sorted out without the spotlight of the news. There has to be that way. The whole opening to China would never have happened ... if Kissinger hadn't undertaken that mission. It would have fallen apart. So you have to use your own judgment." (Henry Kissinger had made secret trips to Red China in 1971 as part of President Nixon's plan to confer legitimacy on the illegitimate Mao Tse-tung regime.)

The main reason for keeping the missions quiet, of course, was to keep the American people from finding out and expressing their outrage at how easily the President could betray the freedom seekers in Red China. The missions sent a message, all right, but it wasn't that the United States was shocked and concerned over the atrocity; it was that the lives of a few thousand young men and women were not as important as diplomatic and business dealings with their murderers.

Appearing before the Senate Foreign Relations Committee on February 7, 1990, Lawrence Eagleburger said that "in the real world, we need to see that China is less completely charming than the land of panda bears and the Great Wall and also less completely evil than a night in June when the 'goddess of democracy' was crushed in Tiananmen." He said that "isolating ourselves from the Chinese people, cutting off the contacts, reducing the dialogue back and forth, will lead to nothing more than an isolated China which returns to the bad old days of a very dictatorial, centralized system that really doesn't care what the rest of the world thinks."

That argument is nonsense, as the International Security Council pointed out in June 1990:

> With regard to "isolation," it is the despotic Beijing regime that has chosen to isolate itself — especially from its own people. On this first anniversary of the Tiananmen Square massacre, it is instructive to recall that the supposedly reformist Deng leadership ordered its tanks to crush the students even as the demonstrations were winding down — and that the protesters were calling for precisely the "liberalization" that Deng's U.S. fan club had claimed was inexorably taking place.

In theory at least, the December trip might have been justified if, for example, clear evidence had confirmed that the massacre was an isolated incident, that the Red Chinese rulers were remorseful over it, and that steps were being taken to bring about democratic changes in the world's largest concentration camp. But the slaughter was not an isolated event; it was rather a typical communist atrocity, like the long list of other atrocities chronicled in *The Human Cost of Communism in China*, to terrorize the people and keep them under control. Deng Xiaoping, who had come to power in 1978, said before Tiananmen Square that "we do not mind spilling a little blood." Like his bloody-handed predecessors, he was not kidding. But bloody massacre or not, it was business as usual, even lying about it, for the Bush Administration.

No Sorrow for Massacre

Was there any remorse on the part of those who ordered the slaughter? Have any fanatical communists ever been sorry for behaving like fanatical communists? Of course not. At a news conference in Beijing on September 26, 1989, Communist Party boss Jiang Zemin, who by the way had a child studying in the United States at the time, said he did not believe that "there was any tragedy in Tiananmen Square. What actually happened was a counterrevolutionary rebellion aimed at opposing the leadership of the Communist Party and over-throwing the socialist system."

As for the future, Jiang said three days later that his forces would "isolate and attack the handful of hostile elements" behind the student demonstrations and resist the "hostile forces, international as well as internal, [that] are still engaged in activities of sabotage and subversion against us."

Less than a month later, on October 2nd, at the headquarters of the Council on Foreign Relations in New York City, Red Chinese Foreign Minister Qian Qichen even ruled out U.S. criticism of the massacre, saying that it was "interference in China's internal affairs." He said that "no one who attempts to pressure China into changing its social system will ever succeed," and that the United States must agree that the "domestic politics of a country should not be taken as a precondition for the restoration and development of bilateral relations." Imagine the reaction if a South African Foreign Minister had tried that argument!

Next it was Prime Minister Li Peng's turn to prove the bankruptcy of the Bush appeasement policy. Addressing the National People's Congress on March 20, 1990, Li applauded the massacre as "China's victory" in foiling "the vain attempt of the international anti-communist and anti-China forces to subvert China's legitimate government and socialist system." He then boldly called for a further crackdown on opponents of the regime:

While fostering socialist democracy and the socialist legal system, we must intensify dictatorship by the socialist state apparatus. Prosecutors and judges should fully perform their duties and be on the alert so that they can promptly crush attempts at infiltration and subversion by foreign hostile forces, and so that they can crack down on all sabotage by hostile elements at home.

In May 1990, Jiang Zemin shocked even Barbara Walters, ABC's ready-to-defend-any-leftist correspondent, when he told her in a television interview that the Tiananmen Square massacre was "much ado about nothing." Jiang said, "I don't have any regret about the way in which we dealt with the events which took place last year in Beijing. I don't think any government in the world will permit the occurrence of such an incident [the pro-democracy demonstrations] as happened in Beijing." He could have added that the Bush Administration had done nothing to cause him to reassess his callous attitude.

Human Rights Abuses

According to Merle Goldman, a professor of Chinese history at Boston University, the post-massacre crackdown referred to by Li Peng was already underway when Scowcroft and Eagleburger visited Beijing in July. Goldman said that "the Chinese began one of their most repressive eras in history — arresting student leaders and the intellectuals who assisted them, brainwashing segments of the urban population and shooting workers. You've really got to question the President's judgment when he would send Scowcroft back, even though there was nothing to show the Chinese were interested in reforming themselves."

When the two Bush representatives were in Beijing in December, police arrested dozens of Roman Catholic priests. "It is a gross insult ... [that] the Chinese turn around and jail priests while they're wining and dining Scowcroft," said John

Davies, president of Free the Fathers, an organization to free jailed clergymen in communist countries. He urged the Administration to halt all loan and trade agreements with Red China. But no such action was taken.

In February 1990, the State Department's annual survey of human rights abuses in all the countries of the world noted that the "human rights climate in China deterioriated dramatically in 1989." The survey said that "the Beijing massacre was followed by a drastic, countrywide crackdown on participants, supporters, and sympathizers. Thousands were arrested, and about a score are known to have been executed following trials which fell far short of international standards." It said that "China rejects the concept of universal human rights" and had "attempted to defend its actions by a massive disinformation campaign, expulsion and harassment of foreign journalists," and a ban on the sale of books by dissidents.

An article in the June 1990 *Reader's Digest*, based on interviews with survivors of Red Chinese prison camps and friends and relatives of those who had disappeared since Tiananmen Square, told what life was like in the "Bamboo Gulag":

> Welcome to your new home. You live in a room with 40 other prisoners. You're not allowed private possessions: no books, no photographs, no keepsakes, no clothes, nothing.
>
> You dig irrigation ditches from sunrise to sunset, seven days a week. When there is a full moon, you work at night too. You come to hate the moon.
>
> Guards don't wait for an infraction to punish you. They tie your elbows behind your back with a wet thong that tightens as it dries. After an hour, you go numb.
>
> The next time, guards push wires through the flesh of your ankles, put an iron band around your skull, and

tighten it until your head cracks. Then they handcuff your arms underneath one leg, raising it tight against your chest. They leave you like that for days, sometimes weeks.

No one escapes from the camp. There's nowhere to go, just sand in every direction for hundreds of miles.

Slave Labor Goods

Forced labor has been the backbone of the Red Chinese economy since the communists captured the mainland in 1949. Today, at least 20 million Chinese, according to some estimates, are being worked to death in thousands of labor camps. Many of the camps have been deliberately located near factories and mines so slave laborers can turn out textiles, chemicals, iron, coal, tools, machinery, consumer goods, and other products. Red China exported $13 billion worth of goods to the United States in 1989. Those Americans who buy items made in Communist China are supporting the regime's slave-labor system.

Actually, U.S. firms importing communist products or investing in Red Chinese industries are breaking the law. Chapter 19, Section 1307 of the United States Code reads as follows: "All goods, wares, articles, and merchandise mined, produced, or manufactured wholly or in part in any foreign country by convict labor or/and forced labor or/and indentured labor under penal sanctions shall not be entitled to entry at any of the ports of the United States, and the importation thereof is hereby prohibited." Needless to say, the law is not enforced. The real question is: Why not?

The slightest concession by the communists is usually grasped at by the U.S. government as justification for significant new ways to help the Reds. For instance, when the Beijing regime announced the lifting of martial law in January 1990, the Bush Administration responded with an easing of its opposition to World Bank loans to Red China. The lifting of martial law was a cosmetic gesture at best — when you have killed or jailed most of your opposition, there is no need for martial law — but President Bush called it "a very sound step."

A.M. Rosenthal of the *New York Times* thought otherwise. At the time the announcement was made, he wrote on January 14th, "many soldiers transferred to the police force, which now numbers more than 1.5 million in addition to an army about twice that size. Laws allowing arrests without explanation, secret trials, executions, indefinite detention without trial, forced labor, press control, brutal student 're-education' camps — all still on the books and recently made even harsher."

But the gesture was enough for Red China's friends in the Administration. In the month of February alone, the Beijing regime received 299,150 metric tons of subsidized U.S. wheat, a $9.75 million loan from the Export-Import Bank to finance the engineering services for a gas processing plant it was buying from McDermott International of New Orleans, a $30 million loan from the World Bank for earthquake relief, and another $23.1 million from the Export-Import Bank for a transportation system in Shanghai that would mean millions of dollars of work for several American companies whose leaders possessed no more scruples than the Bush Administration.

Most Favored Nation Status

President Bush waited until May, however, to give the Reds their greatest reward — renewal for another year of Most Favored Nation trade status, which means it will cost Red China 40 percent less to send the products of its slave-labor system into the United States. "MFN is not a special favor," said Mr. Bush. "It's not a concession. It's the basis of everyday trade. And taking MFN away is one thing I said I would not do, that is, take steps that would hurt the Chinese people themselves. I do not want to do that." He claimed the only message his decision sends is that "isolation is bad and economic involvement is good." The President also expressed his annoyance at members of Congress who "accuse me of being less interested than they are in human rights. I think we're on the right track here."

Several points must be made in response to the President's attempt to justify his abominable policies. First, supplying sustenance of any kind to the Beijing regime is precisely what does "hurt the Chinese people." The same could be said about aiding any tyrannical regime. Next, "economic involvement is good" when it is people-to-people involvement, something that is impossible in the totally controlled atmosphere in Red China where all commerce is government commerce.

Even on our side of these U.S.-Red China transactions, the American people are forced by our government to pay for them with taxes given to the Deng government via the U.S. Export-Import Bank. There is no people-to-people economic involvement in any of this. Regarding "isolation," is it not morally sound to leave isolated a criminal regime that has murdered more innocent human beings than any other in history?

That such points are not constantly raised to demonstrate the moral flaws in the President's policy says a great deal about America's media, the so-called loyal opposition, and even members of Mr. Bush's own political party. The beneficiaries of these flawed attitudes and of the refusal of the Establishment-controlled media to publicize them, of course, are the murderers in Beijing.

In June 1990, on the first anniversary of the Tiananmen Square massacre, the Chinese Reds showed their gratitude for renewed trade benefits by having their military police in Beijing rough up Chinese civilians and foreign journalists, including two Americans who were beaten with rifle butts while trying to cover a protest at Beijing University. The best the State Department could do, as usual, was "deplore the physical abuse and threats of deadly force against journalists engaged in gathering news." Also in June, the State Department confirmed that Red China was continuing to sell poison gas, cruise and ballistic missiles, and other weapons to Iran, Iraq, Syria, and Libya, four of the world's major supporters of international terrorism.

But what does all this matter to a President with no principles, no beliefs, and no moral shame when it comes to building up one of the most depraved dictatorships in history? The long-suffering people of China must surely wish that George Bush's policy toward them was based, as he said in his 1990 State of the Union address, "on a single, shining principle: the cause of freedom." They know that there is nothing kind or gentle about life in the Bamboo Gulag.

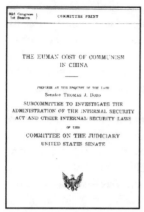

This senate report documented the slaughter of 64 million Chinese.

Lawrence Eagleburger went to Beijing a month after Tiananmen Square.

Communist soldiers using tanks and automatic weapons killed thousands of freedom-seekers in Tiananmen Square on June 4, 1989.

Epilogue

> *President Bush is an intelligent, likable man who handles himself with style but has one important drawback as a player in international affairs. He likes things to be cost-free. When issues of principle get involved that he thinks may interfere with what he wants, he just dumps them. Like, say, supporting the freedom movement in China or standing up to terrorists.*
>
> — A.M. Rosenthal in the
> *New York Times*, June 7, 1990

Criticizing an intelligent and likable man is not the way to win a popularity contest. Americans for the most part are a tolerant people. They are willing to give their President the benefit of every doubt, particularly when he appears to be doing his best. Consequently, anyone who directs criticism his way, even justifiable criticism, is likely to be scorned as an unwanted bearer of bad news. This unfortunate trait of the average American, however, must not dissuade the messenger from shouting his important message from the rooftops — even if the message is contrary to conventional wisdom.

Forty-eight million Americans registered an emphatic decision in the 1988 election when they rejected Michael Dukakis. But those voters thought they were keeping the White House safe from a Democrat who favored bigger government, higher taxes, more appeasement of the communists, and a new world order. Imagine their chagrin on discovering that they had elected a Republican who had adopted the Democratic candidate's agenda. In an Op-Ed piece in the June 7, 1990 *New York Times*, former Dukakis campaign staffers Michael Aronson and Christopher J. Georges expressed their annoyance at the Bush reversal:

> For the past 17 months, President Bush has done what would have been unthinkable during his relentlessly negative 1988 presidential campaign: he has adopted almost verbatim major policy ideas from the campaign of Michael Dukakis. In other words, he has embraced ideas he once ridiculed so successfully when proposed by the "liberal Governor from Massachusetts."

Among other reversals from the Bush campaign oratory, Aronson and Georges cited the President's new support for a ban on certain semiautomatic weapons, elevation of the Environmental Protection Agency to Cabinet status, a halt to oil drilling off the California and Florida coasts, and higher taxes. Governor Dukakis had advocated all of those positions during the 1988 campaign. Doing so in the face of Mr. Bush's opposing views contributed to the Democratic candidate's resounding defeat.

Beliefs of a True Conservative

Although George Bush ran for the U.S. Senate in Texas as a Goldwater conservative in 1964, and has since frequently called himself a conservative, he has seldom acted as one would expect a conservative to act. One sketch of an authentic conservative was drawn by Barry Goldwater in his 1960 book *The Conscience of a Conservative*. Consider some of the basic conservative lines set down by Senator Goldwater and you will likely have a difficult time recognizing George Bush in that sketch.

A true conservative, said Goldwater, is intent on preserving and extending freedom. He is opposed to the accumulation of power in Washington and recognizes that local problems are best dealt with by the people closest to them. He believes that the only "legitimate functions of government" are "maintaining internal order, keeping foreign foes at bay, administering justice, removing obstacles to the free interchange of goods — the exercise of these powers makes it possible for men to follow their chosen pursuits with maximum freedom."

A conservative knows that the founding fathers created a constitutional republic, not a democracy, and that they intended to limit "the federal government's authority to specific, delegated powers." He is opposed therefore to federal involvement in, and would begin a phased withdrawal from, what Goldwater listed as "a whole series of programs that are outside its constitutional mandate — from social welfare programs, education, public power, agriculture, public housing, urban renewal, and all the other activities that can be better performed by lower levels of government or by private institutions or by individuals."

The conservative also recognizes communists as enemies of freedom and therefore considers aid, negotiations, exchanges, and arms treaties with them harmful. "The Kremlin," said Goldwater 30 years before the so-called liberalization of communist Europe, "may, for its own purposes, permit certain 'liberalization' tendencies in satellite countries; it may even permit small deviations from the approved Soviet foreign policy line. It will do so sometimes to confuse the West, sometimes as a prudent means of relieving internal pressures. But it will never let things go too far."

A conservative views the United Nations not as a force for peace, but as "a unique forum for communist propaganda," an organization dominated by communist and other nations hostile to U.S. interests, a financial drain on the American taxpayer, and a vehicle that could lead "to an unconstitutional surrender of American sovereignty."

The people of this country will know they have an authentic conservative candidate for the Presidency, said Senator Goldwater, when he proclaims in a campaign speech:

> I have little interest in streamlining government or in making it more efficient, for I mean to reduce its size. I do not undertake to promote welfare, for I propose to extend freedom. My aim is not to pass laws, but to repeal them. It is not to inaugurate new programs, but to cancel old ones that do violence to the Constitution, or that have failed in their purpose, or that impose on the people an unwarranted financial burden. I will not attempt to discover whether legislation is "needed" before I have first determined whether it is constitutionally permissible. And if I should later be attacked for neglecting my constituents' "interests," I shall reply that I was informed their main interest is liberty and that in that cause I am doing the very best I can.

Beliefs of George Bush

It is difficult to imagine President Bush giving such a speech. He may pay lip service to conservative principles now and then, but his policies are far from conservative. He seems intent on preserving and extending not personal freedom, but rather the reach and power of the federal government into the fields of drug control, the arts, education, the environment, child care, health care, agriculture, energy, transportation — you name it! According to the Constitution, activity in any of those areas cannot be considered a legitimate function of the federal government. In no way can Mr. Bush push the government's nose into all of those tents and still claim to believe in limited constitutional government and decentralization of power.

The same holds true in the area of foreign affairs, where President Bush has praised the sovereignty-destroying United

Nations and fawned over communist dictator Gorbachev. Yes, the Soviet ruler smiles a lot. But every American should recall the 1955 warning of his predecessor, Nikita Khrushchev: "If anyone thinks that our smiles mean the abandonment of the teachings of Marx, Engels, and Lenin, he is deceiving himself cruelly. Those who expect this to happen might just as well wait for a shrimp to learn how to whistle."

Gorbachev has made clear by words and actions that he is a fanatical disciple of Lenin. In a November 1987 speech to his comrades in Moscow, he promised to bring about a "world of communism." In a December 1989 address to a Soviet Congress, he declared himself to be "a convinced communist." And in his own 1987 book, *Perestroika*, he asserted that the purpose of perestroika is to "strengthen socialism." Gorbachev has also solidified his power in the Kremlin and cracked down on Lithuania, while at the same time keeping hundreds of thousands of his troops in Europe and sending military supplies to puppet regimes in Afghanistan and Cuba.

Why would a man like George Bush, who claims to be for freedom, so remarkably befriend a slavemaster like Gorbachev? Why would Mr. Bush go to such lengths to keep the Soviet boss in power? Why would he allow the sale of high-technology products that could eventually be used to fuel the Soviet war machine? Why would he agree to sign more arms treaties just months after telling Congress that the USSR is repeatedly violating previous U.S.-USSR arms accords? Why would he permit his Secretary of State to invite the Soviet Union to send troops into Romania? Which side is President Bush on — the side of freedom or the side of slavery?

As noted elsewhere in this book, he has chosen the side of the slavemasters in Red China and the communist terrorists in South Africa. Granting Most Favored Nation trade status to the Beijing regime after its massacre of thousands of students in Tiananmen Square was an unconscionable betrayal of the

Americanist principles of liberty and justice for all. Rolling out the red carpet for Nelson Mandela in the face of his blatant call for armed struggle, his support for the South African Communist Party, and his avowed friendship with the terrorist trio of Castro, Qaddafi, and Arafat was a severe blow to the aspirations for freedom in the hearts of millions of South Africans — black and white — who do not want to live under a communist or socialist dictatorship headed by Mandela and his comrades.

The Establishment's Man

These and other betrayals make no sense to the millions of Americans who voted for George Bush in 1988 or who gave him such high approval ratings in the polls after his first year in the White House. What would their reaction be if they understood that George Bush is carrying out the agenda of the Establishment, that powerful group of individuals usually found in the ranks of the Council on Foreign Relations and the Trilateral Commission? The Establishment's goal of creating a supranational political and economic system is well documented, notably in James Perloff's book, *The Shadows of Power*, and in Barry Goldwater's book, *With No Apologies*.

These internationalists are "indifferent to communism," said Goldwater. He claimed that, "in their pursuit of a new world order, they are prepared to deal without prejudice with a communist state, a socialist state, a democratic state, monarchy, oligarchy — it's all the same to them." They are interested only in shaping and controlling the global economy and will work with a Gorbachev, a Deng Xiaoping, or a Mandela to gain this enormous power. They care not a whit about preserving such vitally important concepts as freedom, limited government, independence, and national sovereignty.

Does President Bush realize what he is doing? Only he can answer that. Is he aware of what the globalists have in store for a free America? It seems unlikely that he could be unaware. After all, he has been associated with these internationalist movers and shakers for practically all of his adult life, and many of them hold top jobs in his Administration. He has belonged to their organizations until he felt such affiliations would be politically damaging. If the Council on Foreign Relations and the Trilateral Commission were nothing more than the bland "study groups" they claim to be, why did George Bush feel the need to resign from both before making his run for the Presidency in 1980?

The image of President Bush does not correspond with reality, as more and more Americans are beginning to realize. He has offended many of the individuals and groups that supported him in 1988, and his high popularity ratings of early 1990 started declining by the fall, particularly after his reversal on taxes, his effusive welcome for Nelson Mandela, and his planned deployment of 300,000 Americans in the Persian Gulf. This slide in the polls came as no surprise to Richard A. Viguerie and Steven Allen, chairman and communications director, respectively, of United Conservatives of America. Writing in the *New York Times* on June 14, 1990, Viguerie and Allen said that, after spending most of his career as a "country club Republican," Mr. Bush had "restyled himself as a Reaganite to win the Presidency and is now reverting to his old ways." Those "old ways" are the ways of the internationalist and socialist Establishment.

What Is at Stake?

The Bush Administration's agenda is completely inimical to an America founded on the twin beliefs that human beings get their rights from God and that the only legitimate purpose of government is to protect those rights. More than two centuries ago, 56 courageous men pledged their lives, their fortunes, and their sacred honor to preserve and extend the freedoms we take for granted today. Hundreds of millions of individuals have lived and died over the course of human history without ever enjoying those marvelous freedoms even for a moment. Yet many Americans seem unaware or unconcerned that we are rapidly losing what was gained for us at great cost over 200 years ago.

Instead of preserving and passing on the blessings of liberty and morality that we received from earlier generations, we are saddling our children and grandchildren with a monstrous debt, a government big enough to take away their freedoms, and a climate of immorality and degeneracy. What kind of a legacy is that to leave for future generations?

"These are times that try men's souls," Thomas Paine wrote in 1776. "The summer soldier and the sunshine patriot will, in this crisis, shrink from the service of his country; but he that stands it now deserves the thanks of man and woman. Tyranny, like hell, is not easily conquered; yet we have this consolation with us, that the harder the conflict, the more glorious the triumph."

Like our Founding Fathers, we too "live in times that try men's souls." We too find life and liberty threatened by those in power. We too are burdened by the same kind of government oppression that led the signers of the Declaration of Independence to say of King George III: "He has erected a multitude of new offices and sent hither swarms of officers to harass our people and eat out their substance." We too suffer because of Presidents who have left us exposed and vulnerable to enemies bent upon our destruction, and, like King George, have "combined with others to subject us to jurisdiction foreign to our Constitution." And we too have our "summer soldiers and sunshine patriots" who shrink from the sacrifices needed to rescue this great land.

But we also have courageous men and women, young and old, who will not submit to a socialistic new world order; who will defend our God-given rights to life, liberty, property, and the pursuit of happiness; and who will fight for less government, more responsibility, and, with God's help, a better world. This too is a time for patriots. It is a time to get involved in this epic struggle for our humane civilization, a time to remember that "the harder the conflict, the more glorious the triumph."

There are many suffering in slavery today who perhaps often say to themselves, "If only I had known what was happening, there is nothing I wouldn't have done to save my country." If you have read this far, you know what is happening to America. Will you stand by and let our wonderful heritage of freedom be taken from us? Or will you fight to save that heritage so it can be passed along to future generations?

Ponder the words of Joseph Hewes of North Carolina, a signer of the Declaration of Independence who died in 1779, a lonely man separated by his beliefs from his family and friends: "My country is entitled to my services, and I shall not shrink from the cause, even though it should cost me my life." It is to be devoutly hoped that millions of Americans today will not shrink from the cause of preserving that freedom for which Joseph Hewes and his fellow patriots pledged their lives, their fortunes, and their sacred honor. As so many suffering under communist tyrannies have learned, it is not so easy to regain freedom once it has been lost.

The hour is late and the forces of tyranny are moving quickly toward their goal of a one-world socialist dictatorship. And assisting those forces is George Herbert Walker Bush, the 41st President of the United States.

* * *

Patriotism means to stand by the country. It does not mean to stand by the President or any other public official save exactly to the degree in which he himself stands by the country.

It is patriotic to support him insofar as he efficiently serves the country. It is unpatriotic not to oppose him to the exact extent that by inefficiency or otherwise he fails in his duty to stand by the country.

In either event, it is unpatriotic not to tell the truth —whether about the President or anyone else—save in the rare cases where this would make known to the enemy information of military value which would otherwise be unknown to him.

— Theodore Roosevelt

Index

DON'T SIT ON THE SIDELINES!

Here are a dozen good reasons why you should join The John Birch Society.

- A national network of locally functioning chapters all working on a concerted action program.

- A monthly 32-page action and information *Bulletin* going to each member.

- A national full-time field staff coordinating activities.

- A national speakers bureau.

- A national chain of bookstores.

- A national biweekly magazine.

- A national network of ad hoc committees.

- A book publishing arm.

- A video and audio production division.

- A youth program with summer camps and student-run New Americans Clubs on campuses.

- A nationally syndicated newspaper column.

- The private sector's most comprehensive research facilities.

- An active recruitment program constantly converting uninvolved Americans into activists for freedom.

Each of these organizational aspects of our Society is functioning smoothly, and no other group on the scene today even comes close to matching this impressive variety and volume of operations. Any concerned American can't help but conclude that there is a compelling need for what the Society already is — an organization formed to overcome the "nightly network novocain" of television and the generally unreliable perspective given by the rest of our nation's mass media.

The NEW AMERICAN

☐ 3 years (78 issues) $89 ☐ 2 years (52 issues) $68 ☐ 1 year (26 issues) $39 ☐ 6 months (13 issues) $22

Name: _____

Street: _____

City: _____ State _____ Zip _____

VISA or MasterCard #: _____

Signature: _____ Expiration Date: _____

Please address all orders, with payment to:

The New American
P.O. Box 8040
Appleton, WI 54913-8040